Marianna Poutasse

Power of Place

Herman Melville in the Berkshires

Books may be purchased in quantity and/or special sales by contacting the publisher, Berkshire Historical Society at 413-442-1793 or www.mobydick.org

Published by Berkshire Historical Society, 780 Holmes Road, Pittsfield, MA 01201

Designed by Donna Kittredge

Edited by Ellen Garrison

10 9 8 7 6 5 4 3 2 1
First Edition

Printed in the United States of America

ISBN 978-0-9903827-0-6

In memory of my father, J. David Poutasse, an Arrowhead neighbor who also treasured his mountain views in the Berkshires

The Berkshire Historical Society gratefully acknowledges
the support of the following organizations:

CR

ACKNOWLEDGEMENTS

This publication would not be possible without the generous support of the Berkshire Historical Society, the Friends of the Berkshire Athenaeum and the Pittsfield Cultural Council.

I am deeply indebted to Betsy Sherman and Will Garrison at the Berkshire Historical Society for giving me the opportunity to further my knowledge of Herman Melville. It has been a fascinating and challenging task to try to tell the story—in few words—of such an extraordinarily gifted writer and complex man. As a home-grown Pittsfielder myself, I conclude this book with a deeper and more profound understanding of the unique and magnetic pull of the Berkshires on all creative spirits. A special thanks also goes to the amazing and talented graphic designer Donna Kittredge, who I am lucky to call both a great colleague and friend, as we navigated how this book would take shape.

Melville scholar and biographer Hershel Parker's encyclopedic two volumes on Melville were invaluable to me during my research. Special thanks go to Ron Latham, Kathleen Reilly and Ann-Marie Harris at the Berkshire Athenaeum for their research and fact-checking assistance, as well as generous access to and reproductions of images from their collection. To Peter Bergman of the Berkshire Historical Society and copyeditor Ellen Garrison, as well as my friend Victor Jones—who gave the manuscript a good read from a sailor's perspective—I am grateful for your collective critical eyes and insightful comments. Last but not at all least, a huge and heartfelt thanks to my husband Eric, who knew exactly how to hold the boat steady for me as I set sail on this project.

TABLE OF CONTENTS

———

CHAPTER 1

The Family 17

CHAPTER 2

To the Berkshires 31

CHAPTER 3

Wanderings 39

CHAPTER 4

Home from Sea 51

CHAPTER 5

A Move to New York 59

CHAPTER 6

The Summer of 1850 65

CHAPTER 7

A House of His Own 83

CHAPTER 8

Years at Arrowhead 95

CHAPTER 9

A Return to New York 111

The Melville Trail 124

List of Sources 126

CR

INTRODUCTION

In September, 1850, Herman and Elizabeth Melville, with their infant son Malcolm, moved to their newly acquired farm in Pittsfield, Massachusetts. Newspapers throughout New England announced the move: "Herman Melville, the popular young author, has purchased a farm in Berkshire county Mass. . . where he intends to raise poultry, turnips, babies, and other vegetables."

"Arrowhead," named after the Native American artifacts Melville found while plowing his fields, was the Melvilles' home until 1863. It was a place Herman had seen and known since his own childhood visits to Pittsfield. That first autumn seemed a magical time as Herman worked on the farm, settled his extended family into the house, and wrote about whales and the men who hunted them.

The youngest three Melville children, Stanwix, Fanny, and Bessie, were born at Arrowhead, and at various times the house was shared by Melville's mother, Maria Gansevoort Melville, and his sisters, Helen, Augusta, Fanny, and Kate.

Cooking facilities were primitive at Arrowhead, and there was no inside kitchen pump, only an outdoor well. The new kitchen, which contained a sink with an outdoor drain, was separate from the house, perhaps accessible through the porch (or "Piazza") that Melville hired carpenters to build. The carpenters also laid the foundations for several other new outbuildings, including a well house and a wood shed made high enough for Herman to swing an ax indoors for splitting wood.

There were some doubts. Herman's sister Augusta wrote in 1850:

> Our old farm house cannot boast much in point of beauty, but
> it is delightfully comfortable & that is all that is really necessary

This 1870 image of Mount Greylock is virtually identical to the view from Herman Melville's piazza. The outline of the mountain reminded Melville of the shape of a whale, and served as a visual touchstone while he wrote *Moby-Dick*.

Courtesy of The Berkshire Historical Society

in the country. It is an old house, counting its seventy years or more, & though outwardly modernized, retains all its ancient appearance within. It is built after that peculiarly quaint style of architecture which places the chimney—the hugest in proportions—immediately in the center, & the rooms around it. An arrangement so totally void of grace & beauty, must surely possess some counterbalancing advantage, but as yet I have been unable to discover it, even after having made it the subject of the most profound reflection for a fortnight.

But always, the view of Mt. Greylock to the north and the fields and woods closer to home nourished Herman's soul. All figured prominently in several of Melville's writings including the novels Pierre and Israel Potter and the numerous short stories he wrote while living at Arrowhead. His short story, "I and My Chimney," celebrated his special relationship with the environment in which he was living.

It was a relationship filled with adventure, triumph, sadness and ultimately a measure of peace. In this new biography, Marianna Poutasse explores the "power of place," how the Berkshires inspired and sustained Melville, how even after he left Arrowhead and the Berkshires he arranged things so that he never needed to completely leave the place that had often brought him so much personal joy.

As the third of eight children, born in 1819, for his first few years Herman lived a life of privilege. His early publishing successes brought him a fine measure of his future, one that he could not maintain after his move from New York City to the Berkshires. He sold his home to his brother Allan, and after leaving Arrowhead in 1863 his life and his writing talents took him in very different directions once again.

In 1927, Allan Melville's surviving daughters sold Arrowhead. After a succession of private owners, the Berkshire County Historical Society purchased the house and 14 acres in 1975. In 1980, the Society purchased the north field, preserving the view of Mt. Greylock. We are privileged to care for Arrowhead, sharing it with thousands of visitors each year.

This book is the first 21st century commission from the Historical Society. It is a book that we are delighted to present to the public, to Melville fans everywhere, a new look at his life and the true creative power that a place can exert on a talent such as Herman Melville's genius.

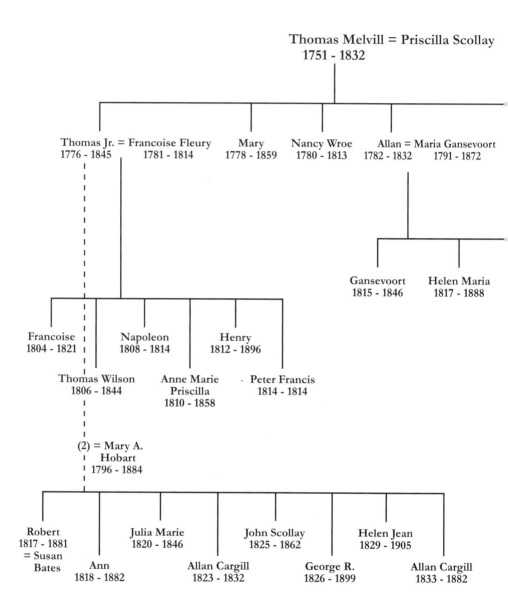

Thomas Melvill = Priscilla Scollay
1751 - 1832

Thomas Jr. = Francoise Fleury   Mary   Nancy Wroe   Allan = Maria Gansevoort
1776 - 1845   1781 - 1814   1778 - 1859   1780 - 1813   1782 - 1832   1791 - 1872

Gansevoort   Helen Maria
1815 - 1846   1817 - 1888

Francoise   Napoleon   Henry
1804 - 1821   1808 - 1814   1812 - 1896

Thomas Wilson   Anne Marie   Peter Francis
1806 - 1844   Priscilla   1814 - 1814
                    1810 - 1858

(2) = Mary A.
     Hobart
     1796 - 1884

Robert   Julia Marie   John Scollay   Helen Jean
1817 - 1881   1820 - 1846   1825 - 1862   1829 - 1905
= Susan
Bates   Ann   Allan Cargill   George R.   Allan Cargill
           1818 - 1882   1823 - 1832   1826 - 1899   1833 - 1882

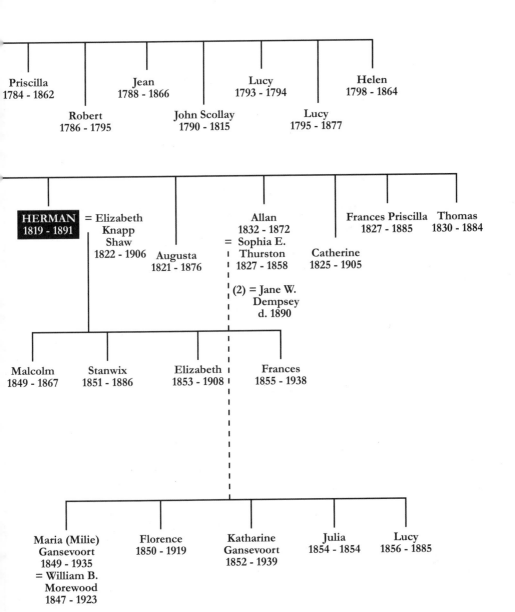

Priscilla
1784 - 1862

Robert
1786 - 1795

Jean
1788 - 1866

John Scollay
1790 - 1815

Lucy
1793 - 1794

Lucy
1795 - 1877

Helen
1798 - 1864

HERMAN
1819 - 1891
= Elizabeth
Knapp
Shaw
1822 - 1906

Augusta
1821 - 1876

Allan
1832 - 1872
= Sophia E.
Thurston
1827 - 1858

(2) = Jane W.
Dempsey
d. 1890

Catherine
1825 - 1905

Frances Priscilla
1827 - 1885

Thomas
1830 - 1884

Malcolm
1849 - 1867

Stanwix
1851 - 1886

Elizabeth
1853 - 1908

Frances
1855 - 1938

Maria (Milie)
Gansevoort
1849 - 1935
= William B.
Morewood
1847 - 1923

Florence
1850 - 1919

Katharine
Gansevoort
1852 - 1939

Julia
1854 - 1854

Lucy
1856 - 1885

This ambrotype of Herman Melville and his younger brother Thomas was taken in Boston before the brothers embarked on a voyage to the Pacific on the *Meteor,* of which Thomas was the captain, in 1860. This is a rare photograph of Herman pictured with a family member.
Courtesy of The Berkshire Athenaeum, Pittsfield, MA

1

THE FAMILY

For most of his life, Herman Melville was surrounded by a large family. He was born the third of eight children in a house that wasn't nearly large enough to give everyone the room they needed. As an adult, not only did his household include his wife and four children, but also his mother, unmarried sisters and a steady stream of visiting relatives and friends. Playing the role of host, husband and father made it difficult to find the peace and quiet needed to write. Melville sought solitary spaces that allowed him to escape into the far reaches of his imagination and craft complex narratives worthy of the great writer he knew himself to be. In the Berkshires, Melville discovered a broad, inspirational landscape that nourished his creative spirit, offered opportunities for solitude in nature and provided the perfect backdrop for a family life in the country.

EARLY YEARS

Born on August 1, 1819, a hot summer day in New York City, Herman was the second son of Allan and Maria Gansevoort Melvill*, a well-bred, aristocratic couple. Their large family would ultimately include four sons and four daughters. The eldest, Gansevoort, was followed in quick succession by siblings Helen, Herman, Augusta, Allan Jr., Catherine (known as Kate), Frances and Thomas III.

In early childhood, Herman and his brothers and sisters were part of

* Members of the Melville family spelled their surname differently; after the death of Allan Melvill in 1832, his wife and children began to spell "Melvill" with a final "e" to become "Melville". Though scholars still debate the reasons for the switch, many posit that the extra letter simply afforded the family an aristocratic flourish that would be useful both socially and in business.

Major Thomas Melvill, Herman
Melville's grandfather, was a
successful Boston merchant
who played a role in the
Boston Tea Party.
*Reproduction courtesy of The Berkshire
Athenaeum, Pittsfield, MA. Original in the
collection of the Old State House, Boston.*

Colonel Peter Gansevoort, Herman Melville's maternal grandfather, was a
wealthy Dutch landholder in upstate New York. He played an important
role in the defense of Fort Stanwix during the American Revolution. The
Gansevoort family crest (left).
All images courtesy of The Berkshire Athenaeum, Pittsfield, MA

the privileged upper class, living among other wealthy New York families in fashionable lower Manhattan. The Melvills moved occasionally, usually to larger accommodations with better addresses, and each of their large, handsome houses was furnished elegantly and maintained by a collection of servants. The Melvill brood was always under the watchful eyes of various nurses and tutors. Like other well-to-do families, Herman's parents put a high value on their children's education, and as a young child Herman attended both the New York Male High School and the Grammar School of Columbia College.

Each of the Melvill boys was raised with great expectations for his professional and social success, and the girls would, in due course, enter society as refined and suitable prospects for marriage. As they grew and matured, all the children were also keenly aware of their distinguished ancestry on both their father's and mother's sides of the family. The Melvill and Gansevoort clans' long-rooted and powerful social and political connections all but assured the children's own successes throughout their lives.

FAMILY TIES

Allan Melvill's father, Thomas, was the son of a wealthy Scottish immigrant who graduated from Princeton University in 1769 and became a successful merchant in Boston. Thomas Melvill was swept up in the Patriotic fervor leading up to the American Revolution. In late 1773, he joined the Sons of Liberty in the famous Boston Tea Party, disguising himself as an American Indian, boarding a British vessel and dumping an entire shipment of tea from the East India Company in the Boston Harbor. During the war, Melvill was an officer in artillery units in Boston and Rhode Island. After the war, George Washington appointed him Inspector of Customs, a coveted post that was renewed by subsequent presidents until 1811 when President Madison named him as Naval Officer for the District of Boston and Charleston. Melvill's grandchildren treasured their occasional visits to their patriot grandfather, where they could revel in his tales of the Boston Tea Party, and admire his riding boots, which still had tea leaves tucked into their cuffs.

Maria Gansevoort Melvill's background was equally impressive. She was born in Albany, where her family was highly esteemed as one of the earliest Dutch families of upstate New York. Her first cousin, Stephen Van Rensselaer, was the 8th and last "Patroon" landholder in New York, one of the wealthiest men in America with powerful rights and privileges. Additionally, she was

Herman Melville's father, Allan Melvill, painted by John Rubens Smith at the height of his business success, circa 1810.

closely related to other major Dutch founding families, including the Ten Eycks and Van Schaicks. Like Thomas Melvill, Maria's father Peter Gansevoort had also served bravely in the American Revolution. Colonel Peter Gansevoort, in command of the 3rd New York Regiment of the Continental Army, defended Fort Stanwix during a 21-day siege by the British Army. Strategically located near present day Rome, New York, Fort Stanwix and its defenders prevented the eastward marching British troops from reinforcing their comrades along the Hudson River. This contributed to the Americans' crucial victory at the Battle of Saratoga in late summer 1777. Herman and Maria Melville named their second son Stanwix in honor of Col. Gansevoort.

A FATHER'S FALL FROM GRACE

Allan Melvill was raised with every prospect to achieve fame and fortune. With their revolutionary fame and wealth, the Boston-based Melvills were held in high esteem by the tastemakers of Boston society. As a young man, Allan fit into that scene with perfect ease and comportment. At the conclusion of a Grand Tour of Europe, which he chose in lieu of attending university, Allan settled in Paris with his older brother Thomas, Jr. Allan quickly embraced the European taste for fine luxury goods and within a short time, determined to make his mark as a gentleman merchant in the import and export business. After establishing strong relationships with dry-goods suppliers in Paris, he returned to America with the intention of settling in Boston among his family and friends, and using his social connections and good breeding to build a distinguished clientele.

From the very outset, however, Allan struggled to succeed. He had refined and expensive tastes, but very little business sense, and had difficulties convincing conservative Bostonians to spend their money on the latest fashions from Paris. New York, on the other hand, offered a better chance for business and for the Melvills' social lives. It was certainly a more cosmopolitan city, and had a wider range of deep-pocketed and socially climbing individuals with penchants for expensive European goods. In a letter from Paris informing his family of the move to New York, he explained, "I have been induced by the advice of my commercial Friends here & at home, & various important personal considerations, to establish myself permanently at New York, a City of unexampled growth & prosperity, & of unrivalled local resources & foreign intercourse, which must become the great Emporium of the western World—my acquaintances there are numerous and respectable, and my Wife's

Maria Gansevoort Melvill, Herman's mother, painted as a young woman, circa 1826.

Maria's mother, Catherine Van Schaick Gansevoort, circa 1826.
Images top left and right, courtesy of The Berkshire Athenaeum, Pittsfield, MA

Allan Melvill brought this cup and saucer from Paris as a gift to his father. The pieces are adorned with the family's crest.
From the Herman Melville Collection at The Berkshire Athenaeum Photo by Eric Korenman

Family and Connexions [sic] who are among the first People in the State, (the Gansevoorts & Van Schaicks, of dutch [sic] extraction,) will afford me the same consideration I enjoy in my native town."

By 1817, the young couple had set up housekeeping in a large brownstone in lower Manhattan, and Allan was reestablishing himself "on a permanent & respectable foundation" in the city. His optimism was premature, however, for throughout the next fifteen years, as the Melvill children arrived one after another at nearly two-year intervals, the nation plunged into a deeply rooted recession, with frequent bank failures and business foreclosures. Potential customers were often short on cash, and creditors loomed. Additionally, Allan had a difficult time understanding—and thus competing with— an emerging group of young, shrewd entrepreneurs who had discovered a more cut-throat way to buy and sell goods in the competitive and depressed market.

Over these years, Allan repeatedly begged and borrowed heavily from his wealthy father, as well as close family friends. When he could, he also aggressively tapped into his wife's Gansevoort and Van Schaick family resources, which largely took the form of advances against her inheritance. With his aristocratic pedigree, fluency in French and confidence in his refined tastes, he pressed on; more than once he entered into questionable business partnerships and investments. Continuing to make trips back and forth to Europe for more goods, Allan remained almost blindly optimistic that his personal integrity and quality goods would, sooner or later, result in a profitable business. "Though Fortune has played me many a scurvy trick, I will not complain of the fickle Goddess, who may yet be inclined to smile graciously upon me."

At home in New York, Maria tended to the growing number of children at her heels, and with a strict and officious manner, kept her seemingly prosperous household running as smoothly as she could. The house was full of European furniture, exotic objects d'art, huge portfolios of French prints and hundreds of leather-bound books including work by Racine, Voltaire and Rousseau, which gave every suggestion that the family was privileged and financially secure. Behind this façade of good living, however, Allan faced mounting debts to his family and friends that were increasingly irresolvable.

Major Thomas Melvill had been extremely generous in his advancements to his son, both in fronting money to purchase goods and to pay off debts, but as a proud and thrifty New Englander, he had no intention of letting his son's poor business sense and reckless borrowing destroy his estate

> "...little Herman...[is] very backward in speech & somewhat slow in comprehension, but you will find him as far as he understands men & things both solid & profound, & of a docile & aimiable disposition..."
>
> —Allan Melvill describing Herman at age 7

and impact his other children's inheritances. In a clause of his will dated February 1829, Major Melvill announced "...whereas I have lent and may hereafter lend to my son Allan considerable sums of money, for which I have taken or may hereafter take his promissory notes, or other security, it is hereby declared that all such sums are to be considered debts due to my estate." Thomas Melvill would not allow his increasingly spendthrift son to bring shame on the entire Melvill family.

Maria Melvill's widowed mother, Catharine Van Schaick Gansevoort, shared similar concerns about her son-in-law's ability to manage his accounts. While Allan had appealed to his wife's brother, Peter, for assistance, and had also already dipped into her inheritance, Catherine had carefully and quietly taken notice. In her will dated June 1830, Catherine clearly spelled out a plan to protect Maria from her husband's financial peril, indicating her executors to "pay the income and profits of one equal fourth part [of the interest on bonds] thereof to my daughter Maria during her natural life for her separate use; free from the debts and control of her said husband."

Thomas Melvill and Catherine Van Schaick Gansevoort's admonishments came true within a year. In the early fall of 1830, the Melvill family's world came to a stunning crash, when Allan was forced to liquidate his business, cancel his lease and pack up his young family and their furniture, sending them to Albany to seek refuge with Maria's family. Herman, who was just eleven years old, stayed behind in New York with his father, helping tie up loose ends. By October, father and son left New York for good, traveling up the Hudson River under the cover of night so as to avoid attracting the attention of any creditors looking for them. It was a precipitous fall from grace, and one that would affect Herman profoundly for the rest of his life.

EARLY YEARS IN ALBANY

Maria's Gansevoort family offered assistance and advice, but only from arm's length, as they were completely disgraced by her husband's financial situation. Maria's brother Peter, who felt a certain responsibility for his sister, was troubled by her circumstances, but neither he nor any of the Gansevoorts permitted Allan, Maria and the children to live with them. Instead, Allan was forced to find humble accommodations for his family and take work as a clerk, a far cry from his previous position as a gentleman merchant.

In the shadow of Maria's rich extended family, the Melvills tried to keep up appearances despite their circumstances. They enrolled the three eldest sons, Gansevoort, Herman and Allen, Jr., at the Albany Academy, with the expectation that the boys' education would remain a top priority. While the three were old enough to understand their family's precarious financial position, they must have been grateful to continue their schooling and mingle with boys from well-heeled families who might not have been aware of the Melvills' bleak situation at home. Numerous letters exchanged between family members clearly reflect that the first-born Gansevoort was the most promising and favored son. Though "little Herman," as he was affectionately known by the family by the age of seven, was "an honest hearted double rooted Knickerbocker of the true Albany stamp," his father also noted that he was "very backward in speech & somewhat slow in comprehension, but you will find him as far as he understands men & things both solid & profound, & of a docile & aimiable [sic] disposition..." A few years later, in the summer of 1831 at the age of twelve, Herman surprised his family by distinguishing himself as a promising student. Achieving the highest marks in arithmetic, he was awarded first premium in his class, and a copy of *The London Carcanet, Containing Select Passages from the Most Distinguished Writers* (New York, 1831) with an inscription from the principle of the Albany Academy "To Herman Melville [sic]/The first best in his class/in ciphering books./T. Romeyn Beck, Principal."

Under exhaustive pressure to work long hours at a middling job and finding himself unable to repay the debts he owed to so many, Allan Melvill's mental and physical health declined dramatically over the years in Albany. He died at age forty-nine on January 28, 1832. He left his wife and the eight children deeply in debt to countless creditors and family members or friends who had extended themselves over the years. Records show that at the time of his death, Allan owed the New York State Bank alone the enormous sum of $19,000. Over the coming years, Maria would spend countless days in court trying to settle her husband's business affairs, while simultaneously appealing to her family, particularly her successful brother Peter Gansevoort, for financial assistance.

Allan's death would have a deep and lasting effect on all the children. Being the eldest, Gansevoort was immediately propelled into a life far from academics: a quick-paying profession that would help support his family. For the second son, Herman, education had become an unaffordable luxury, and he faced an uncertain future. In his novel *Redburn*, Melville would reflect back on his tumultuous childhood, admonishing his reader to "Talk not of the bitterness of middle-life and after life; a boy can feel all that, and much more, when upon his young soul the mildew has fallen; and the fruit, which with others is only blasted after ripeness, with him is nipped in the first blossom and bud. And never again can such blights be made good; they strike in too deep, and leave such a scar that the air of Paradise might not erase it." Allan Melvill's death and the family's subsequent disgraced position was profoundly soul-wrenching and incalculably damaging to Herman.

TO WORK

At age sixteen, Gansevoort suddenly found himself in the unfortunate position of being the oldest male in the Melville household, with an expectation to provide for his family. The weight of responsibility rested heavily on his shoulders, and Herman no doubt also felt immense pressure to earn an income. Fortunately, Peter Gansevoort felt a duty to help his widowed sister's family, and used his connections to broaden his nephew's job prospects in Albany. Just months after her husband's death, Maria withdrew Gansevoort from the Albany Academy, signing a memorandum "…to certify that my son Gansevoort Melvill, is carrying on the Fur and Cap business in the City of Albany, on my account, and that I hold myself responsible for all debts contracted by my said son, in the course of said business." It was promising employment, as Albany was quickly becoming a hub of the country's commercial industry. The opening of the Mohawk and Hudson Railroad in 1831 had provided an efficient way to ship lumber, grain and fur, and the completion of the Erie Canal in 1825 had further opened up trade and expansion as far as the Northwest Territories. Gansevoort had a real chance of making a living and he jumped into it full-force.

Within just a few months of establishing the fur and cap business for Gansevoort, Uncle Peter also made arrangements for Herman to find employment. At just twelve years old, Herman accepted a job as a clerk at the

Herman Melville's older brother, Gansevoort, at age 16.

New York State Bank, a position for which he would earn $150/year. It was a job he would hold for nearly the next three years, working long hours six days a week. He undoubtedly felt angry about his fate and captive to his position. In "Loomings," the first chapter of *Moby-Dick*, Melville describes how the men not destined for a life at sea still craved Sunday afternoon walks along the docks of Manhattan, the one day free "...of week days pent up in lath and plaster—tied to counters, nailed to benches, clinched to desks."

In Albany, Gansevoort quickly proved to be a well-spoken and solid businessman, one who knew how to make strong connections for his business throughout the state and beyond. With a fierce determination to take his family out of debt, he worked tirelessly. In addition to the rigors of setting up a business, Gansevoort also had the heavy burden of working alongside his mother to try to settle some of his father's seemingly endless debts, while aggressive creditors from Boston and New York relentlessly tried to collect a portion of their loans.

To make matters worse, Allan Melvill's father Major Thomas Melvill died shortly after his son. Almost immediately, Allan's surviving siblings banded together in a lawsuit against Maria and her children, in order to protect their own inheritances from his creditors. Though it was a legal necessity to do so, Maria could not help but feel it a complete betrayal and rejection of her and her children. "Oh the loneliness the emptiness of this world when a woman has buried the husband of her youth & is left alone to bring up their children, without a loved father's care & experience in the training them to fulfill life's duties & to point the way to heaven by his Christian example," she wrote in reflection years later. Herman and his siblings suffered equally, as Melville would later write in *Redburn*, "I must not think of those delightful days, before my father became a bankrupt, and died, and we removed from the city; for when I think of those days, something rises up in my throat and almost strangles me."

SELF-IMPROVEMENT

Despite the family's crippling financial situation, both Gansevoort and Herman harbored glimmers of hope for a better future, and looked for opportunities to continue their educations and enrich their intellects. Both boys were voracious readers, and as early as 1834 Gansevoort had gained access to at least one circulating library. In Albany, both Gansevoort and Herman frequented John Cook's reading room, the Athenaeum Library and the library at the Albany Academy. The two also joined the Young Men's Association for Mutual Improvement, which was open to any men from the ages of sixteen to thirty-five "without distinction of pursuits, profession, or calling," according to a scrapbook description now in the Albany Public Library. The Association had a large "Periodical Room," and Gansevoort recorded spending significant hours attending debates with audiences that he described as "large & respectable." Within a

> "I must not think of those delightful days, before my father became a bankrupt, and died, and we removed from the city; for when I think of those days, something rises up in my throat and almost strangles me."
> —Melville, in his novel *Redburn*

short period of time, Gansevoort began participating in the debates, likely aware of the professional and social advantages of sharpening his public speaking and debating skills. Herman also later join the Philo Logos Society, a debating club "formed for the purpose of improvement in composition, elocution and debate."

Even as Gansevoort and Herman put forth their best efforts of hard work and self-improvement, things took another dramatic turn for the worse in 1834, when the factory where Gansevoort's goods were produced was devastated by fire. Unable to pay his employees, nor provide them with a place to work, Gansevoort released everyone from employment. Devastated at his inability to provide either for his employees or for his family, Gansevoort decided Herman should leave his post at the New York State Bank immediately, and instead join him in the cap and fur business. Herman had to go with some resentment about being pulled from a secure, paying job at the bank. He would stay at work with Gansevoort for the next three years, until Gansevoort's business went bankrupt in 1837.

To this point, Herman's childhood had been marked by a series of hardships and disappointments—his father's death had set off a chain of unfortunate events that had to affect him deeply. Being pulled from school, then removed from steady employment at the State Bank, only to have his brother's once-promising business fail, there was little happiness for the eighteen-year old as he faced his next decade.

An image of Park Square, Pittsfield, Massachusetts, circa 1835.

The Berkshire House was located in the center of Pittsfield. Guests of the Melville family stayed at the hotel during the summer of 1850.
Both images courtesy of The Berkshire Athenaeum, Pittsfield, MA

2

To the Berkshires

As Maria Melville and her children encountered setback after setback, there was one cherished, idyllic place where they found a welcome respite from the ever-present burdens of their financial position. Maria's brother-in-law, Thomas, Jr., who as a young man had lived in Paris, had ultimately settled in the foothills of Western Massachusetts in the town of Pittsfield.

During the summer of 1832, Maria brought all eight of her children with her to Pittsfield, a relatively easy 45-mile journey, when an outbreak of cholera swept through Albany. With eleven hundred cases reported and four hundred people having succumbed to the highly infectious bacterial disease, Maria was anxious to get out of town and fled quickly. As daughter Helen wrote three weeks later, "We left Albany so suddenly that I hardly realized our departure until when arrived here I was surrounded by cousins most of whom I had never seen and assailed on all sides by the clamorous din of no less than 17 children."

A Brief History of Pittsfield

Escaping the city by stagecoach, Maria set foot in Pittsfield at a time when the once agrarian village was rapidly shedding its rural character, emerging as a small but budding cosmopolitan New England town. Due in large part to economic entrepreneurs like Arthur Schofield, who introduced the first carding machine for wool in 1800, and Elkanah Watson, who introduced Merino sheep to fellow Pittsfield residents in 1807, Pittsfield was fast emerging as a leading center of woolen manufacturing. Other industries, such as paper making, and businesses like the Berkshire Mutual Fire

Melvill Place was a well-known local landmark on the South Road, one mile south of the center of Pittsfield. Today it is the Country Club of Pittsfield.

The large center hall mansion had two double parlors for large-scale entertaining.

Both images courtesy of The Berkshire Athenaeum, Pittsfield, MA

Insurance Company (1834) and Berkshire Life Insurance Company (1851) also provided employment for the growing population, and consequently, the number of shopkeepers, tavern keepers, blacksmiths, tanners and other businesses grew as the community prospered.

Census records indicate that the Pittsfield population in 1820 was 2,768, but by the eve of the Civil War, that figure jumped dramatically to 8,000. Between the years of 1840 and 1850 alone there was a 57% jump in the population. Textile mills and other businesses were quick to hire newly arrived Irish, French Canadian and other immigrants who came specifically to Western Massachusetts in search of work.

Pittsfield was situated squarely in the center of Berkshire County, and in 1837 became the central hub for all railroad service within the Berkshires, connecting to Albany, New York and beyond. The railroad provided Pittsfield residents and other Berkshire consumers with access to a wider selection of fashionable and practical goods. Local merchants like Moses England, who opened his first dry goods store on the east side of North Street in 1857, relied on the railroad to build their businesses and their clientele. As importantly, train service offered an increasing number of visitors and tourists an efficient, easy and pleasant mode of travel to and from the region.

THE MELVILL PLACE

In 1816, Major Thomas Melvill purchased an elegant house and large farm in Pittsfield along the South Road for his eldest son and namesake, Thomas, Jr., who had returned to America from Paris after the death of his wife Françoise Lamé-Fleury. He secured a lucrative contract to feed British prisoners at a frontier outpost in Pittsfield during the War of 1812, and at the conclusion of the war, Thomas, Jr. decided to settle permanently in the western Massachusetts town, hoping to pursue the life of a gentleman farmer there along with his second wife Mary Hobart Melvill. Like his younger brother Allan, Thomas, Jr. always seemed to struggle professionally and financially, and relied heavily upon his father's substantial post-Revolutionary wealth. Though he had made a handsome fortune in the war, after repaying his father a $14,000 loan. Thomas, Jr. had very little left over to foot the bill for a suitable property, and Major Melvill provided the resources for his son as he had done so often for both his boys.

That property, a well-known local landmark, was first owned by former Albany postmaster Henry Van Schaack, who had purchased 246 acres in about

1780 and almost immediately built an elegant, grand Dutch colonial mansion. The second owner, wealthy businessman Elkanah Watson, was another Albany transplant who came to Pittsfield in 1807 with a serious interest in sheep and cattle farming. Watson was keen to develop the property into a model farm and breed Spanish Merino sheep, known to produce the softest and finest wool. By the time the property fell to the care of the Melvills, the fame of the first two owners, coupled with its imposing location along the well-traveled road to Lenox, made it well-known in Berkshire County. The house may have shown some age by the time Maria and the children arrived for their visit in 1832, but its grandeur was still firmly intact, with a broad center hall perfect for entertaining, wainscoted rooms finished with imported French wallpaper and furnished with an impressive European and American furniture, paintings and decorative details.

THE SUMMER OF 1832

Although at first glance Maria may have found her brother-in-law's rural lifestyle somewhat unrefined, she was grateful to have an escape from the infectious city she left behind, and the change of scenery was a welcome distraction from her situation at home. Despite any temporary misgivings, within days the charms of country living took hold of her. "The family are very kind, the Children live on bread & milk, look brown & healthy—all have gain'd flesh, & my baby Tom is the picture of plenty & good nature. The air is delightful, we literally breathe sweets, the atmosphere is fill'd with fragrance from the new-mown hay, all around us, Gansevoort is employed, in raking & turning Hay, Fishing, rowing the Ladies across, & around a large pond back of the house, & in doing ample justice to the excellent Milk & delicious bread & Butter of the Farm we are happy here, but would wish to return to town as soon as would be prudent." The stunning mountain views, fresh air, picturesque farmlands and simplicity of day to day life was intoxicating to Maria and all of the children. The family thought of it as a kind of escapist paradise far from all the grit, clamor and harsher realities of a more urban life in Albany.

Although most of the family would remain in Pittsfield for the entire summer, Herman's visit was brief, due to his obligations back at the bank in Albany. But for the short while he could enjoy the break, Herman discovered that a country life suited him immensely. He embraced farm chores as a welcome change from the confines of monotonous work at the bank and discovered he loved being outdoors and working with his hands. The informal

Thomas Melvill, Jr. came to Pittsfield during the War of 1812. He settled
with his family at Melvill Place. This miniature was painted in Paris,
circa 1800.

From the Herman Melville Collection at The Berkshire Athenaeum

Photo by Eric Korenman

life led by his uncle, aunt and cousins was infinitely more attractive to him than the rigid, proscribed life at home. Herman joined his siblings and cousins swimming in the Melvills' large pond at the eastern part of the property, developed a love of taking long, rambling hikes in the surrounding countryside or going strawberry picking in the fields down by the limestone quarry.

Herman also loved spending time with his eccentric but affable uncle. Reveling in Thomas, Jr.'s stories of living in Paris as a younger man, when he served as acting American consul in France, Melville reminisced that his uncle was "Mild and kindly, with a faded brocade of old French breeding." He described that his well-bred aristocrat-turned-farmer, when working in the fields would "at times pause in the sun, and taking his smooth-worn box of satin-wood, gracefully help himself to a pinch of snuff, partly leaning on the slanted rake, and making some little remark, quite naturally, and yet with a look, which—as I now recall it—presents him in the shadowy aspect of a courtier of Louis XVI, reduced as a refugee, to humble employment, in a region far from the gilded Versailles."

Thomas, Jr. farmed his land employing many of Watson's progressive farming methods, but by and large the work was unprofitable. He was deeply in debt throughout the 1820s, and brought shame upon the family by spending months in a debtors' prison in nearby Lenox, the county seat. Despite these failings, Thomas, Jr. still remained an esteemed member of Pittsfield and the larger Berkshire community. He won the plowing contest at the Berkshire Agricultural Fair in 1818 and was elected president of the Berkshire County Agricultural Society in 1835. The following year his farming talents were celebrated when he was the "first to introduce the Ruta Baga within the County." He also served on the town's school committee, and was an impressive amateur artist, teaching his children and nephew how to draw.

From his first visit during the summer of 1832, Herman fell deeply in love with Pittsfield, the Melvill Farm and the way of life it provided. Although work at the bank and later at Gansevoort's cap and fur store always beckoned, the Berkshires sparked something deep inside Herman from a young age, and he would return to Pittsfield and the Berkshires again and again to refuel his spirit and soul.

FARMING, TEACHING AND OTHER PROSPECTS

Ultimately, Thomas, Jr. decided to leave Pittsfield. In June 1837, after struggling to make ends meet for years, he and his son John determined to head west towards Galena, Illinois. Leaving the farm in the care of his eldest son, Robert, Thomas was optimistic that in Galena they would find steady jobs and be able to have the rest of the family join them there soon. Herman spent the summer in Pittsfield, helping his aunt Mary and cousin Robert with the hard work of running the farm. He became physically stronger by working the land, and increasingly independent. As his cousin Julia remarked to Maria, "He is very good very polite. You need not feel uneasy about him we will try not to make him quite a savage while he resides in the country as you fear we shall."

With no real job prospects on the horizon back in Albany, Herman found a position as a teacher in the Sikes District School, located in the southeast corner of Pittsfield on Washington Mountain, a "remote & secluded part of the town about five miles from the village." He took board at an isolated house "on the summit of a savage and lonely mountain," with a man described as the "perfect embodiment of the traits of Yankee character,--being shrewd bold & independent, carrying himself with genuine republican swagger, as hospitable as 'mine host' himself, perfectly free in the expression of his sentiments, and would as soon call you a fool or a scoundrel, if he thought so—as, button up his waistcoat.—He has reared a family of nine boys and three girls, 5 of whom are my pupils—and they all burrow together in the woods—like so many foxes." But the setting was "...most splendid & unusual...".

The position did not last long, and Herman reluctantly returned home the spring of the following year. Having a hard time making ends meet in Albany, Maria had since moved to Lansingburgh, a small town just north of the city. There she rented a house on the Hudson River that looked out to a busy commercial scene of lumber barges and other commercial vessels passing by at regular intervals. Herman, meanwhile, took a course in surveying and engineering at the Lansingburgh Academy, with the hopes of ultimately securing a job on the Erie Canal, using connections provided by his uncle Peter Gansevoort. Between 1836 and 1840, it is likely that he took on work as a hired man from time to time, but his efforts for a more professional position were completely unsuccessful. While he waited for another promising opportunity, he began to write short pieces for the local papers. Herman Melville launched the beginning of his writing career on May 4, 1839 with a serial publication for *The Democratic Press and Lansingburgh Advertiser* entitled "No. 1" of "Fragments From A Writing Desk." Though Allan Melvill had once indicated that his second son was slow to read and write, Herman was now discovering he had a voice for storytelling.

A view of the Liverpool Harbor. This is a scene Herman would have
encountered upon his arrival in 1839.
Courtesy of The Berkshire Athenaeum, Pittsfield, MA

From the painting *Panorama of a Whaling Voyage Round the World* by Benjamin
Russell and Caleb Purrington depicting the harbor in New Bedford,
Massachusetts.
Courtesy of the New Bedford Whaling Museum

3

WANDERINGS

C *all me Ishmael. Some years ago - never mind how long precisely — having little or no money in my purse, and nothing particular to interest me on shore, I thought I would sail about a little and see the watery part of the world. It is a way I have of driving off the spleen and regulating the circulation. Whenever I find myself growing grim about the mouth; whenever it is a damp, drizzly November in my soul; whenever I find myself involuntarily pausing before coffin warehouses, and bringing up the rear of every funeral I meet; and especially whenever my hypos get such an upper hand of me, that it requires a strong moral principle to prevent me from deliberately stepping into the street, and methodically knocking people's hats off - then, I account it high time to get to sea as soon as I can. This is my substitute for pistol and ball. With a philosophical flourish Cato throws himself upon his sword; I quietly take to the ship. There is nothing surprising in this. If they but knew it, almost all men in their degree, some time or other, cherish very nearly the same feelings towards the ocean with me.* —From the opening of Moby-Dick

After futile attempts to land a position on the Erie Canal, Herman began to feel that life in Lansingburgh was increasingly claustrophobic, especially when sharing the cramped quarters of the two-family house with so many siblings and his strong-willed and often domineering mother. Maria constantly fretted about money, and suffered bouts of depression and anxiety about her family's position. For a young man of twenty, the urge to get out and away from his present situation—no matter how—was an alluring prospect, and he ached to do something novel and exciting.

A reliable (though not entirely respectable) choice for a young man without a solid education was to go to sea. Herman sought advice from his cousins Leonard Gansevoort and Thomas W. Melville, who had both served brief stints on whaling ships, and was immediately enthralled by their tales of distant lands and adventures on the high seas. Though his older brother and mother would have preferred that Herman pursue a more disciplined and distinguished career in the U.S. Navy, the temptation to do something daring beckoned.

Herman's immediate choices were to sign on either to a merchant ship or a whaler. Neither would earn him much money to help support his struggling family, but he soon made up his mind to enlist as a cabin boy aboard the *St. Lawrence*, a small, three-masted, square-rigged merchant ship making a four-month journey from New York to Liverpool. In addition to a huge cargo of cotton earmarked for the mills in Manchester, Birmingham and Leeds, an advertisement that appeared in the *Evening Post* indicated that the ship also carried cabin and steerage passengers "handsomely accommodated at low rates."

From the moment the ship set sail on June 4, 1839, Herman was filled with excitement. As he later recounted in *Redburn*, "Every mast and timber seemed to have a pulse in it that was beating with life and joy; and I felt a wild exulting in my own heart, and felt as if I would be glad to bound along so round the world." His day-to-day work—whether swabbing the decks, rigging the sails or cleaning out the pig pens and chicken coops—was physically demanding but he took to it easily, without complaint or regret.

Arriving at Liverpool nearly a month later, Melville was astounded at the city's bustling commercial wharves, lined with vessels as far as the eye could see. There was also an eye-opening racial diversity in the crowds, and he was struck by the enormous and extremely visible gaps between the rich and poor; more than a third of the city's population lived in slum-like conditions. With guidebook in hand, Herman spent his days away from the ship as a tourist, taking in Liverpool's historic sights, wandering the town's large avenues and myriad side streets, and trying to soak up absolutely everything he could on this first trip to Europe. When he returned to the Port of New York in late September, it was clear that his voyage on the *St. Lawrence* was to be just the beginning of his wanderings at sea.

A RETURN TO LANSINGBURGH

If the newly minted sailor thought things at home would have changed for the better during his four months away, Herman was to be severely

Herman's mother rented this house in Lansingburgh, New York shortly after the death of her husband, Allan. It is now the home of the Lansingburgh Historical Society.

Courtesy of The Berkshire Athenaeum, Pittsfield, MA

disappointed. Instead, he arrived at Lansingburgh to learn that his mother's financial situation was even more dire, as her landlord was threatening to cancel her lease. Though her third son Allan, Jr. was working and provided some money for the family, and her brother Peter and other family members extended modest assistance, Maria still felt panicked by her situation. When she was ordered to sell her furniture to pay Gansevoort's back debts on his cap and fur business, she pleaded that "It cannot be possible that I am to be left by my two Brothers to struggle with absolute want, or be compelled to write painful truth-speaking letters, descriptions of our situation, to ward of[f] by a reluctant remittance, our present wants—*and how that is done*, by paying off every cent I receive to pay those I owe & in a few days to be poor again, untill necessity once more compels me to the same disagreeable duty—I can hear you say the times are hard, tis true—if I could postpone my wants until the times become easy, I would do it with all my heart." She implored further that "Shelter, food, & fuel, cannot be postponed—neither Shoes nor the wearing of them to those in the habit of wearing them."

Herman knew he needed to do his part to help his mother, especially given the fact that Gansevoort, who was always thought of as the most promising of all her children, was suffering from an undiagnosed chronic pulmonary illness and unable to lessen his mother's burden. In the fall of 1839, Herman quickly signed on to his second teaching job, at the nearby Greenbush & Schodack Academy, located in East Greenbush, New York. This establishment was more sophisticated than the Sikes school where he had taught briefly just two years earlier in Berkshire County, and Maria was hopeful that the position would earn Herman enough to provide her with between $150 to $200 a year, a sum she desperately needed to help defray her own expenses.

At the conclusion of each school week that winter, Herman returned to Lansingburgh. Trudging home through snow and sleet-covered roads, he braced the bitterly cold, 15-mile journey to save what little he could on room and board. It was a short-lived solution, however, for by the early spring of 1840 the trustees of the school informed him of impending bankruptcy and could no longer pay his wages.

Once again, Herman pondered an uncertain future with looming family responsibilities gnawing at him. With an increasing agitation to flee his present and seemingly hopeless situation, it did not take long to set his sights on another adventure, this time heading west to Illinois, just as his

Uncle Thomas and cousin John had done a few years earlier. In the company of an old school chum named Eli James Murdock Fly, Herman imagined that the trip to the edges of the American frontier would, at the very least, promise some sort of employment, and at best lead him to find a fortune out in the West—a prospect always so far out of reach back home. After the long journey, however, Melville and Fly arrived in Galena to find Uncle Thomas to be in no better a financial position than he

> "...if I could postpone my wants until the times become easy, I would do it with all my heart. Shelter, food, & fuel, cannot be postponed— neither Shoes nor the wearing of them to those in the habit of wearing them."
>
> —Maria Melville

had left back in the Berkshires years before. Herman quickly realized how the economic depression that had plagued the east was now making its trek aggressively westward, leaving few job prospects in its wake, especially for a young man with just a modicum of teaching experience and surveying skills. It was only a matter of months before Fly and Melville packed their bags and returned to New York.

Life there was no better. Feeling socially disgraced, debt-ridden and desperate, Maria's now nearly constant pleas for assistance were beginning to go unheard. "Oh that the Lord may strengthen me to bear all my troubles, & be pleased to sustain me under them…I feel unusually depressed & troubled, and cannot throw it off. I feel as if my poverty & consequent dependance [sic], have robbed me of the affection of my dear brothers, at a time when true love & Friendship is alone to be tested, *in adversity*…"

To Whaling

After living and working on a merchant ship and seeking fame and fortune in the west, Melville had developed an unshakeable wanderlust—one that would only be satiated by signing on to a much bigger and infinitely more dangerous adventure. The whaler *Acushnet* was scheduled to embark on a four-year journey to the South Pacific on January 1, 1841 from Fairhaven, Massachusetts. It seemed to offer the perfect escape Herman had dreamed of since childhood. Taking him to exotic reaches of the globe and freeing

Hunting whales was a gruesome, exhausting and dangerous occupation.

One of the prints in Melville's extensive collection was an engraving after a watercolor by Clarkson Stanfield.

him from both his oppressive family circumstances and the stifling social and professional expectations he had thus far failed to meet, the prospect was intoxicatingly appealing. He could completely lose himself at sea. The trip would, with any luck, be the turning point in his life. "Having little or no money in my purse, and nothing particular to interest me on shore, I thought I would sail about a little and see the watery part of the world," his character Ishmael would later explain in *Moby-Dick*.

Seafaring was respectable when one pursued a naval career, but there was little to celebrate when a son chose to be a common sailor aboard a whaling ship. The dangers of such an experience were also immense—stories of shipboard mutinies, run-ins with fierce behemoth whales bent on destroying their captors, tumultuous seas insured that no one signed on without an understanding of the huge risks involved in such a voyage. In the company of a salty and potentially dangerous crew, which might include drunkards, fugitives, rovers and other societal outcasts, life onboard could be risky itself. Melville shared the company of twenty-six shipmates, including four Portuguese, three black Americans, one Scotsman, one Englishman and a handful of white Americans who could trace their ancestry back to other countries. They would all live and work in close quarters, doing chores, telling tales, and spending day after day counting the hours until a bellowing call of a whale sighting from the mast set off a flurry of preparations for a gruesome, long, messy and exhausting kill.

An 1829 article appearing in the *Washington Daily National Intelligencer* succinctly describes life on a whaler during the middle years of the 19th century.

> Those who have never taken the trouble or never have had an opportunity of visiting a whale-ship, fitted for a three years' cruise beyond Cape Horn, will be ignorant of what they have lost, until a leisure moment is profitably employed in that way. There, between the plank and timber of a ship of four hundred tons, is a little world; a monarchy in miniature, with an Emperor whose power is absolute as that of the Moon's twin brother who reigns in China, and with occupations as various are to be found in a house of industry.

Signed on as a "green hand," Herman's payment, called a "lay," would be set at 1/175th of the total profits of the voyage. This was not a money-making venture in any sense, and the money he was advanced against his pay to equip himself with necessities left him with nothing more to send home at the beginning of the journey.

The *Acushnet* traveled south around Cape Horn by April 15, continued up the coast of Chile and reached the Pacific Equatorial whaling grounds by the summer of 1841, some six months after it set sail from Fairhaven. After a full year at sea, the whaler turned west toward the Marquesas Islands, one of the most remote groups of islands in the world. Anchoring at Nuku Hiva in the summer of 1842, Melville and his crewmates were awestruck by the island's beauty, though mindful of the formidable presence of six French vessels in the harbor, indicating that the islands had recently been taken under French control. The moment the whale ship pulled into harbor, nearly naked local young girls swam out to welcome the new visitors and offer themselves to the men as they wished, a customary greeting for all ships entering the islands. It must have felt like pure nirvana for the crew of the *Acushnet* who had been at sea for so long, in the company of only men and without chance of female companionship for months or years at a time.

Intoxicated by the tropical beauty, the surfeit of young women and a craving to escape the harsh conditions on board ship, when Herman and his co-conspirator Richard Tobias "Toby" Greene went ashore on July 9th, they had already hatched a detailed plan to desert the whaler. They intended to spend a short time exploring the island's terrain, and then sign on to another ship. It was a dangerous gamble. Captains could usually rely on natives to be ruthless informers, exchanging a captured deserter for cash. On board, deserters were put in irons and lashed repeatedly. Melville and Greene worked quickly, however, and successfully disappeared deep into the mountainous terrain, leaving no trace or trail to follow.

They would spend the next several weeks with the natives of the famous Typee tribe, "a fierce and unrelenting tribe of savages" as Melville describes them in his book by the same name. Usually heavily tattooed, the Typee were famous among whalemen for cannibalism, and Greene and Melville must have been concerned for their safety. To complicate matters, at some point during their escapade Melville suffered an injury to his leg that left him lame, and Greene set out on his own to find help. When he failed to return, Melville found himself utterly alone among the exotic tribe, no doubt suspecting that his luck among them might run out soon. Whatever initial

Richard Tobias Greene, Melville's fellow seaman on the
Acushnet. The pair jumped ship in the Marquesas Islands
in July 1842
Courtesy of The Berkshire Athenaeum, Pittsfield, MA

concerns he had, however, over the next few weeks the foreigner was treated kindly by the Typee; they even successfully treated his lame leg.

Melville decided to gently extricate himself from the tribe and decamp from the remote islands by signing on to another vessel docked at Nuku Hiva called the *Lucy Ann*. With ships coming and going from ports regularly, it was not difficult to climb aboard, if one was willing to endure the hard labor and absolute rule of the captain and his crew. The *Lucy Ann* was an Australian whaleboat that thus far had had little luck, having taken only two whales since it left its Sydney port. It had also lost twelve of its original thirty-two crewman to desertion. Melville was probably a welcome addition, though he would find that its volatile and often drunken skeleton crew was in shambles, overseen by a mad, tyrannical captain.

As if all of his adventures in the South Pacific to date were not astonishing enough, a further chain of events unfolded for Melville once he was at sea. Shortly after shipping out from Nuku Hiva, the motley crew staged a mutiny against their captain, and Melville and the rest of the men were jailed by the British consul in Tahiti. Fortunately security was lax, and prisoners were allowed to roam freely during the day as long as they returned for evening lock up and agreed to sit in the stock if the jail was under inspection. One day after daytime release, Melville simply drifted off. He soon picked up short-term work as a farm hand. By October of 1842, he had signed on to yet another vessel, the Nantucket whaler *Charles and Henry*.

By May, the twenty-three-year-old Melville found himself in Hawaii a free man—free from shipboard or family obligations and completely adrift, perfectly content to live a rogue life for awhile longer, with no immediate intention or yearning to make his way home. Honolulu was still considered a faraway port, but it brimmed with sailors and ships from all over the world. Melville would have the opportunity to hear headlining news from the States, especially the devastating and widely discussed story of the U.S.S. *Somers* mutiny. His cousin Guert Gansevoort, a once esteemed 2nd Lieutenant in the Navy, had been one of the officers who had hastily found two fellow midshipmen guilty, sentencing them to death by hanging at sea from the ship's yardarm. It was a chilling reminder that life at sea was dangerous for every man, no matter his ranking.

Melville soon grew tired of his life on the run, and left Hawaii in August by signing on to the US Navy frigate *United States* as an ordinary seaman. As the frigate set out from Honolulu, with its first anchor to be put down back in the Marquesas Islands, the boisterous chatter among the crew was undoubtedly laced with the same sort of rumors of cannibalism and scantily clad island women that Melville had been privy to before. As a repeat visitor, Melville was in the perfect position to captivate his audience, spinning clever and amusing yarns and enthralling the crew. All evidence suggests that by this time, Melville would have certainly begun to realize that his series of adventures—from the *St. Lawrence* to the *Acushnet,* to the *Lucy Ann, Charles and Henry* and finally the *United States*—were storytelling pearls that could be strung together into one great adventure: a story about whaling, beachcombing, living among cannibals, sexual licentiousness, mutiny—a tale like none other yet in existence.

Reaching American shores in October 1844, Melville set foot on dry land at the Navy Yard in Charlestown, Massachusetts—four-and-one-half years after his odyssey at sea had begun. He was a physically, emotionally and intellectually changed man, already calculating his next adventure. But this time, the adventure would unfold in his imagination, with pen in hand.

Elizabeth "Lizzie" Shaw Melville, circa 1847.

Chief Justice of the Massachusetts Supreme Judicial Court Lemuel Shaw, Herman Melville's father-in-law.
Both images courtesy of The Berkshire Athenaeum, Pittsfield, MA

4

HOME FROM SEA

With a thick, heavy beard and rugged demeanor, Herman Melville stepped back into American society completely transformed. The once soft-spoken second son was newly born as a handsome, swashbuckling adventurer. After so much time away, Melville was anxious to get home to Lansingburgh to reconnect with his mother, sisters and younger brother Thomas. He also had thoughts of making his way further south to New York City, where Gansevoort and Allan Jr. had set up a promising law office. But for a short time the former sailor docked in Boston, acclimating to life on land by embracing the richness of city life that he had all but forgotten at sea. He also visited a few aunts and old family friends, among them the Shaws of Beacon Hill.

Lemuel Shaw had been a close friend of Melville's father, Allan, and had once been engaged to Allan Melvill's sister Nancy, who died suddenly before the marriage could occur. A wealthy and highly esteemed lawyer who built a large and thriving practice in Boston, Shaw also had the dubious distinction of being the co-executor of Major Thomas Melvill's estate. The position required him to navigate the often treacherous waters between warring sides—on one, Allan Melvill's siblings, who wanted to be protected from the crushing debts he left behind in the wake of his death in 1832—and on the other his widow Maria, to whom Shaw felt beholden, especially because she was left so financially and socially bereft. Shaw was a former member of the Massachusetts House of Representatives, a state senator from 1821-22 and had been awarded the coveted appointment of Chief Justice of the Massachusetts Supreme Judicial Court in 1830, a post he would hold for thirty years.

> "Do not go out in the Evening with young men, but stay at home & study, go to bed early, be pure in mind, think finely, remember that from the 'heart proceeds all evil & learn to keep you heart with all diligence."
>
> — Maria Melville's advice to her sons

In his private life, not only did Shaw suffer the loss of his fiancé Nancy Melvill, but also his first wife Elizabeth Knapp, who died during childbirth, leaving him to single-handedly care for their young son, John, and newborn daughter, Elizabeth, affectionately called Lizzie. Shaw was a widower for nine years before he married Hope Savage Shaw in 1827, and the couple had two more sons.

When the twenty-five year old sailor arrived at the doorstep of the Shaw's elegant three-story brownstone on Mount Vernon Street, he likely cut an impressive figure to both his father's old friend as well as Shaw's eligible daughter, Lizzie. During Herman's time at sea, Lizzie had become a dear friend to Herman's sisters, especially Helen, and the pair had spent long stretches of time visiting at each other's homes in Lansingburgh and Boston. Lizzie felt close to the Melvilles, and was excited to be reacquainted with the young man she knew from childhood visits between the two families.

Even if Lizzie caught Herman Melville's eye on his visit, he was still anxious to reunite with his family, and soon said his goodbyes as he left Boston for Lansingburgh. Settling in to the very different tempo of daily life in upstate New York, Melville was eagerly embraced by his mother, sisters and younger brother, and kept everyone fascinated and entertained with rich tales of his extraordinary life at sea and among the so-called cannibals of the Typee tribe. Enthralled by his storytelling abilities, the family encouraged him to put the tales down on paper.

A BUDDING AUTHOR

Melville was coming to the same conclusion on his own. He would not merely set his sights on writing installments for a newspaper, as he had done before he went to sea, but instead aimed to write a bigger, more serious book about his travels. He envisioned the book not only as a travelogue documenting his escapades, but also as a platform on which to discuss topics that had become important to him since setting sail, when he had experienced first-hand the evils of colonialism, cultural biases, missionary zeal, slavery and imperialism. It was a tall order, but he was confident and excited to get to work.

Maria Melville was delighted to have her son at home, and in her own way, shared her children's pride and delight in their brother's new persona. Ever anxious about her own situation, which had largely settled down to a middle class lifestyle thanks in part to income from Allan, Jr.'s law practice and small family inheritances, Maria was still eager for Herman to earn a proper living that might boost her social position further. In the fall of 1844, Melville set up a simple study among the eaves of the attic in Lansingburgh and began plotting out his first real book, to be based on his time among the Typee.

Although some writing began in Lansingburgh, Melville also made his way down to New York during the late fall of 1844 and the winter months of 1845, finding his brother's law office a suitable space free from family distractions and his mother's constant oversight and meddling. Overprotective and worried that her grown boys would be led astray by city living, she admonished them, "Do not go out in the Evening with young men, but stay at home & study, go to bed early, be pure in mind, think finely, [and] remember that from the 'heart proceeds all evil & learn to keep you heart with all diligence.'"

Though he might not have heeded his mother's advice completely, Melville did set down to work, and soon completed the manuscript for his first book, entitled *Typee*, readying it for submission to the New York publishers, Harper & Brothers by late spring. Dedicated to close family friend Lemuel Shaw, Melville had every expectation that the book would be accepted, printed and quickly become a must-read sensation. Much to his surprise, Harper & Brothers summarily dismissed it, claiming that it seemed so far-fetched, so outrageous in some of its scope, that it simply could not be based on truth. Melville was furious and would hold a grudge against the publishers for years to come. As a niece later recalled, "One thing I do know, the Harpers refusing it calling it a second "Robinson Crusoe' embittered his whole life."

Fortunately, Gansevoort encouraged his brother to give him a copy of the manuscript before he set sail for London, where he had just secured a coveted position as Secretary to the American Legation. Gansevoort sent the manuscript to the English publisher John Murray, who quickly agreed to take it, even if he considered some parts good fiction rather than strict truth. Gansevoort also showed proofs of the book to author and diplomat Washington Irving, who recommended it to the American publishers Wiley & Putnam as part of their *Library of American Books*, a series edited by Evert A. Duyckinck. By March 1846, Melville's *Typee*, or as it was fully known in America, *Typee: A Peep at Polynesian Life During a Four Months' Residence in a Valley of the Marquesas*, was in print on both continents, and Melville was soon hailed as a new American author to watch. Evert Duyckinck reviewed the book for the New York *Morning News* declaring it "a happy hit whichever way you look at it, whether as travels, romance, poetry or humor," with "a sufficiency of all of these to be one of the most agreeable, readable books of the day." For those who criticized it as being scandalous, unfair in its portrayal of American missionaries in the Pacific, and most importantly overtly fictitious, the sudden appearance of Melville's old shipmate friend Toby Greene, who had not been seen nor heard from since leaving Melville on the Marquesas Islands, was an incredible surprise. Living in Buffalo, New York, Greene happened to see a review of *Typee* disparaging Melville, and immediately penned a letter to the local paper verifying that "I am the true and veritable 'Toby,' yet living, and I am happy to testify to the entire accuracy of the work, so long as I was with Melville." This proved to be a publicity bonanza, and the man who lived among the cannibals, a veritable "Typee" himself, was an overnight sensation in the public's eye and his book an immediate best-seller.

With almost manic intensity and amid all the publicity over *Typee*, Melville immediately began to pen his second book during the winter months of 1846. He had hit his stride as a writer, and planned a sequel to his first book, to pick up the story when Greene and Melville left the Typee and signed on to other whalers. *Omoo* would be loosely based on facts but also full of fictional details. In May, while working at break-neck speed on the manuscript, Melville received news of Gansevoort's sudden death in London. Though distraught and shaken, he doggedly charged ahead with his writing. As a second son, he had never imagined he would need to act as a breadwinner for the family, but with Gansevoort's passing, he was put exactly in that role, and the intensity of the realization set him to work with an even greater fervor.

Omoo appeared in print both in London and New York by the spring of 1847. While there had been speculation that a sequel to his first book might be inferior, reviewers were gratified to find *Omoo* "lively, sparkling, humourous, conversational, diversified with little episodes of ocean life and vivid descriptions of southern scenery." A small regional English paper, the *Nottinghham Review and General Advertiser for the Midland Counties*, called it "just one of those works which, once commenced, so fascinates the reader, that he finds it difficult to lay it down until he has devoured every page," and went on to claim that it was "destined to become as great a favorite with the adventure-loving public" as *Typee*. As a budding celebrity, Melville was also appearing with increasing frequency on the social pages of newspapers far and wide as an attractive and eligible suitor, a rogue adventurer turned literary rock star with a growing following of young women vying for his attention.

ENGAGEMENT AND MARRIAGE

Since their initial meeting in Boston, Lizzie Shaw and Herman Melville had many opportunities to see each other. Lizzie was a regular visitor to Lansingburgh since he had returned home, and her stays provided ample time to get to know each other better. In addition to the usual daily family interactions—meals, gathering in the parlor or taking leisurely walks—there were also social obligations in and about Lansingburgh, and Melville would have been a proper gentleman to escort Lizzie about town, arm in arm. She was just three years younger than he, and her life to date was decidedly more privileged, sheltered and proper than Melville's had been.

Judge Shaw raised Lizzie with every advantage—from 1835 to 1841 she attended the Progressive School for Young Ladies, which offered girls a course of instruction equal to that more commonly given to boys. Lizzie was well schooled in English, Latin, arithmetic, science and history, and her education prepared her for college at the Mount Holyoke Female Seminary or Oberlin College. Though she chose not to attend either one, her rigorous education was impressive for a young woman of the 1840s. In addition to her studies, Lizzie was a skilled pianist, an avid and talented rider, and she loved to dance. She was clever, an excellent writer and voracious reader, with a passion for discussing books and ideas in depth. Melville was attracted to her on all these levels, but perhaps it was her adoration of him—and his writing—that made her even more attractive. The ties between the Melvilles and Shaws also provided a natural bond from the start, and Lemuel Shaw was fond of Melville, even if he had reservations about how such a young man with no foreseeable prospects in business could support a wife and family by his writing. Melville recognized this shortcoming, and for a time tried to pursue a more stable

> " *...if it were to get about previously that 'Typee' was to be seen on such a day, a great crowd might rush out of mere curiosity to see 'the author,' making it very unpleasant for us both.*"
>
> — Lizzie Melville on why the couple was married at home

job as a customs or a government official that might be acquired through family connections, but to no avail. By the beginning of 1847, Herman intended to marry Lizzie, though he had not yet proposed. At the time, he was at work on what would be his third book, *Mardi*, and his mother Maria found her son to be "very restless and ill at ease and very lonely without his intended."

Lizzie accepted Melville's proposal later that spring, and her father finally agreed to the engagement. Excitement within the family and among the society pages was immediate and abundant. Helen, who cherished both her brother and her dear friend exclaimed, "Herman has returned from a visit to Boston, and has made arrangements to take upon himself the dignified character of a married man sometime during the Summer...I can scarcely realize the astounding truth!" A newspaper columnist declared "Herman Melville, Esq., author of 'Typee' and 'Omoo,' we are happy to learn is likely to find more happiness in civilization than he ever enjoyed in the romantic Valley of the Marquesas. We expect to find the full particulars in a few days under the proper head, in some Boston paper."

On all fronts, it appeared to be the very best of unions. For Maria Melville, it was a proper and financially advantageous joining of two families, and for her daughters it brought a cherished friend into the family fold. By all accounts, the reading public greeted with enthusiasm as well as surprise the news that the rogue adventurer had decided to cease his wandering and settle down.

Lizzie and Herman were wed on August 4, 1847 in the formal parlor of the Shaws' elegant brownstone on Beacon Hill. Though the couple had originally intended a church ceremony, they made a last-minute decision to be married at home, because as Lizzie explained "if it were to get about previously that 'Typee' was to be seen on such a day, a great crowd might rush out of mere curiosity to see 'the author,' making it very unpleasant for us both." On the day of the wedding, Herman found a four-leaf clover and presented it to his fiancé as an indication of their good fortune, and it was ceremoniously placed in the family bible. Family legend holds that Herman presented his wife with a new four-leaf clover at every anniversary for years to come.

After a honeymoon up through the White Mountains of New Hampshire and into eastern Canada, then back down along Lake Champlain, Herman and Lizzie returned to Lansingburgh. For a time, they would share cramped quarters with Maria and several of Herman's sisters who were still living at home. Though Lizzie would have preferred to set up her own housekeeping, she deferred to Maria Melville at every turn, given Maria's tendency to be domineering and interfering. It was not an easy situation for the newlyweds.

The Melvilles' building no longer stands, and there are no known images.
The New York City brownstone buildings pictured here, built in the 1840s,
are very similar.

Courtesy of Christopher Gray, MetroHistory.com

5

A MOVE TO NEW YORK

It did not take long for Herman and Lizzie to find their new life together woefully restrictive, living under the formidable wing of Maria Melville. Lansingburgh was also provincial, and Herman quickly decided that he wanted to live in New York City, which would put him at the center of a well heeled, fashionable and literary circle. Allan Melville, Jr., and his new wife Sophia were also house hunting in New York, and the brothers decided to join forces and lease a large brownstone on Fourth Avenue between Eleventh and Twelfth Streets. It was a situation Melville could not afford on his own, but was made possible with financial backing from Judge Shaw, coupled with a steady income provided by Allan's earnings as a lawyer and assistance from Sophia's father. By October 1847, the brownstone not only housed Herman, Allan and their new brides, but also became almost as crowded as Lansingburgh had been when Maria, Helen, Augusta, Kate and Fanny moved in. The youngest, Thomas, had set his sights on a life at sea, and was far from the stressful dynamic of the large extended family that revolved around Maria and her every wish on Fourth Avenue.

If Herman was overwhelmed by a household full of women, he was fortunate that Evert A. Duyckinck's residence, which included an impressive private library of over 16,000 books, was located just a stone's throw away on Broadway. Duyckinck regularly invited Melville to socialize and peruse the shelves of his vast collection, which spanned an enormous range of topics from classical literature to Shakespeare, philosophy and art. Melville read voraciously. He was buoyed by the friendship, and Duyckinck was equally excited to introduce his new author to all the right circles of people—leading New York intellectuals,

> Lizzie worried as her husband locked himself away for hours on end, without eating or drinking, emerging hours later tormented with exclamations, "Oh Lizzy!—the book!—the book—what will become of the *Book*!"

writers and artists. Gatherings at the home of Dr. John Wakefield Francis were enticing, and Melville described them as the "center for the intellectual galaxy of this metropolis."

Herman had very little interest in larger, more public social engagements and unless in the company of fellow intellectuals or artists, was happier at home. Often secluding himself to write for long stretches of time, he worked tirelessly on his third book, *Mardi*, which he hoped would mark a shift in his reputation from travel and adventure to serious literature. He approached writing *Mardi* with bouts of manic intensity, and was consumed with the idea to create something less straightforward than his earlier *Typee* and *Omoo*. The new work would be laced with allegorical subtleties and political commentary.

Lizzie worried as her husband locked himself away for hours on end, without eating or drinking, emerging hours later tormented to exclaim, "Oh Lizzy!—the book!—the book—what will become of the *Book*!" Writing was all-consuming and exhausting to him both mentally and physically, "for while Herman is writing the effect of keeping late hours is very injurious to him—if he does not get a full night's rest or indulges in a late supper, he does not feel bright for writing the next day and the days are too precious to be thrown away—and to tell the truth I don't think he cares very much about parties either, and when he goes it is more on my account than his own. And it is no sacrifice to me, for I am quite as contented, and more—to stay at home so long as he will stay with me."

Despite the chaos of so many family members living under the same roof, coupled with the annoyance of always having to defer to her often rigid and opinionated new mother-in-law, Lizzie quickly settled into a routine. In a long and detailed letter to her stepmother on December 23rd, 1847, she provides an extraordinary description of her new life.

> We breakfast at eight o'clock, then Herman goes to walk,
> and I fly up to put his room to rights, so that he can sit down

to his desk immediately upon his return. Then I bid him good bye with many charges to be an industrious boy, and not upset the inkstand, and then flourish the duster, make the bed, &c in my own room…then ding-ding goes the bell for luncheon. This is half past 12 o'clock—by this time we must expect callers, and so must be dressed immediately after lunch. Then Herman insists upon my taking a walk every day of an hours length at least…By the time I come home it is two o'clock and after, and then I must make myself look bewitchingly as possible to meet Herman at dinner…At four we dine, and after dinner is over, Herman and I come up to our room, and enjoy a cozy chat for an hour or so—or he reads me some of the chapters he has been writing in the day. Then he goes down town for a walk, looks at the papers in the reading-room &c, and returns about half past seven or eight. Then my work or my book is laid aside, and as he does not use his eyes but very little by candle light, I either read to him, or take a hand at whist for his amusement, or he listens to our reading or conversation, as best pleases him. For we all collect in the parlor in the evening, and generally one of us reads aloud for the benefit of the whole. Then we retire very early—at 10 o'clock we are all dispersed—indeed we think that quite a late hour to be up.

The letter illustrates Lizzie's dedication to her author husband, how she was supportive of his need for seclusion during the writing process, but also acted as an interested and encouraging confidant to discuss the developing narrative. When not tending to his needs, Lizzie was a capable housekeeper who could balance the demands of the household and the social obligations of being an author's wife and New York society woman equally well. She also understood Melville's temperament—his need for a rigid writing schedule, requirements for daily walks along the wharves or the Battery to clear his mind, and a household that adjusted to his routine. One of Lizzie's most important roles, along with his sisters Augusta and Helen, was to serve as a copyist to Herman, which required transcribing his messy and frenzied handwriting into a neat, more readable format. In a letter to her mother, Lizzie apologized for careless punctuation, as she had become accustomed to not inserting punctuation because Melville preferred to do his own on the final copies of his work.

GETAWAYS TO PITTSFIELD

At the first signs of spring in 1848, when Herman felt New York was becoming too confining, he left the city alone for a trip to Pittsfield, where he could escape both the torment of his writing and his family, which was increasingly too close for comfort on Fourth Avenue. Although he intended to arrive to the first buds of spring, he found himself hunkered down in the midst of a late-season snowstorm. Renting a room in town, he visited the beloved Melvill Place, where his cousin Robert and his family were struggling to keep the old estate running. He also spent time with his cousin Priscilla, who was the daughter of Uncle Thomas and his first wife, Frenchwoman Françoise Lamé-Fleury. Priscilla's mother died when she was a young child, and although she had an impressive, aristocratic French pedigree from her mother, she had never left Pittsfield and lived meagerly, barely making ends meet as a seamstress.

Priscilla and Robert were both eager for the rest of the Melville family to reunite at the farm the coming summer. In writing to her cousins with an invitation, Priscilla fondly recalled the Melvilles' childhood trips to Melvill Place, advocating that "…the return of summer would certainly bring you to your senses, & to Pittsfield…but you must allow for the difference between our bracing mountain air—& the soften'd atmosphere that surrounds you in the city—." Despite the recent snow blanketing the Berkshire hills, "it will very soon wear a more attractive appearance & you will be tempted to leave the home that possesses so many charms at present to enjoy for a season the pleasures of the country."

Though there is no evidence that the entire Melville clan took Priscilla up on the offer, Herman and Lizzie decided on a brief holiday to the Berkshires in August. Pregnant with their first child, Lizzie would have welcomed a break from the heat of the city (and her mother-in-law) and the opportunity to get some time alone with her husband. But when they arrived at Melvill Place, Lizzie and Herman learned that in an effort to stay solvent, Robert had made the decision to rent rooms in the house to boarders seeking a summer vacation. He had advertised in the local *Pittsfield Sun*

THAT FINE OLD MANSION known as the Melvill House, situated one mile south of the Village of Pittsfield, Mass., having been put in order for the accommodation of persons who are desirous of spending the summer months in the country, the subscriber would say to such, that they can hardly fail to be pleased with the House or its situation. The rooms are very large, with many conveniences not usually found in ordinary boarding houses, and the situation is unrivalled either for the beauty of its scenery or the salubrity of the air. A carriage will be in attendance for those who may wish to avail themselves of the many pleasant drives in the vicinity.

The Pittsfield farm attracted a distinguished clientele. Summertime boarders included famed poet Henry Wadsworth Longfellow and his wife Fanny, who spent much of the month of July at what they described as "Melville Hall, Typee Valley," a mansion as comfortable and lovely as their own beloved Craigie House in Cambridge. Fanny exclaimed "We have a grand old mansion here, in the style of ours, with immense halls, a porch in front & a stoop with blinds behind, built by a wealthy Dutchman of Kinderhook. It is very spacious & comfortable, & very well kept by Typee's cousin, an intelligent farmer." Longfellow enjoyed the rolling pastures and meadows, and lyrically referred to the lake on the property as "the Tear of Heaven."

Melville ventured to Pittsfield in April and August, both times restless and agitated by the confines of the city, his household and his writing. Since his childhood, Pittsfield had been a precious place and it remained so for him as an adult—he still cherished his rambling walks and hikes, the chance to work on the farm doing gardening and chores, as well as the overall easier pace of life in the country, which gave a fresh perspective on his life and on his work. In short, Pittsfield was the perfect tonic for what ailed him. During the April visit, Priscilla wrote that Herman "has manifested so much constancy toward the object of his first love our Berkshire farm—as to tear himself from the idol of his heart to indulge again in the unfetter'd freedom of Batchelor [sic] days". She is the first to document Melville's strong feelings for the Berkshires and the family estate, and her words set the stage for his next visit and ultimate move within just two years' time.

A daguerreotype of Elizabeth Shaw Melville with her first child,
Malcolm Melville, circa 1850.

Courtesy of The Berkshire Athenaeum, Pittsfield, MA

6

THE SUMMER OF 1850

B y the first half of 1850, Allan and Herman Melville's New York household had grown to include two children. Herman and Lizzie were now the proud parents of a one-and-a-half-year old son, Malcolm, and Allan and Sophia's daughter Maria, known as Milie, was also underfoot. Grandmother Maria still ruled the roost, and Herman's sisters Helen, Augusta, Kate and Fannie all still remained at home, making social calls, writing letters and making occasional excursions to Albany and Boston. Behind the scenes, several servants and a nanny kept the house running smoothly, especially as Herman secluded himself in his study for long bouts of writing.

Published in 1849, *Mardi* proved to be a less successful book in comparison to *Typee* and *Omoo*, and did not sell well. While some reviewers found it to be ambitious and majestic in its prose, others were less enthusiastic, describing it as lofty and self-indulgent. A reviewer for the *Boston Post* called it "a mass of downright nonsense," while another hailed it "a rubbishing rhapsody." Feeling the financial and professional pressure to keep his career on track, Melville quickly penned two more sea narratives, *Redburn* and *White-Jacket*, and disparagingly described them to his father-in-law Judge Shaw as "two *jobs*, which I have done for money—being forced to it, as other men are to sawing wood." He was clear in writing them that "my only desire for their 'success' (as it is called) springs from my pocket, & not from my heart." Referring to the failed *Mardi*, which he considered a work of genius, he explained, "So far as I am individually concerned, & independent of my pocket, it is my earnest desire to write those sorts of books which are said to 'fail.'—Pardon this egotism."

Melville remained confident in his writing, but was increasingly frustrated that he was not deriving much income from it and had to increasingly rely on regular cash infusions from Judge Shaw to keep the family living in the manner to which they were now accustomed. In October 1849, Melville set sail for Europe, resolved to hand-deliver the manuscript for *White-Jacket* directly to his London publisher Richard Bentley. He anticipated that in person, he might secure a more advantageous contract with Bentley both for the book and a handsome advance. He was hoping to offset expenses for a several months' long Grand Tour, and the advance from Bentley would enable the exhausted author a long-overdue respite from the intensity of writing three books in under two years, and might also provide more material for future work. But Bentley had lost a great deal of money on *Mardi*, and in their meeting was not convinced that sales of either *Redburn* or *White-Jacket* would be strong enough to warrant an advance. Without money in his pocket, Melville's Grand Tour was cut woefully short, and he returned home much sooner than anticipated.

At sea for the several weeks' long trip back to New York, Melville had time to reflect on his work thus far and ponder his next steps. He was undeterred by recent lackluster book sales and unfavorable reviews, and began crafting an idea for yet another book—his sixth—which would take the form of an American whaling story full of tragedy and drama unlike any sea narratives yet in existence. Back at home in the city, Melville delved deeply into his own memories of his seafaring days for material, and voraciously devoured books about whaling, natural history and geography. During the early months of 1850, a steady stream of books fueled the author, who secluded himself in his study for long stretches of time, shutting out his family and the world to focus on his writing. The story of the whale known as Moby Dick was pouring fast and furious from the tip of his pen. Although his previous work had not launched his career as far as he had hoped, he remained convinced that this next book would undoubtedly be the great turning point of his career.

By June of that year, Melville was confident the book would be ready by the coming autumn, and wrote to Richard Bentley to propose publishing it in London. He described his latest venture as "a romance of adventure, founded upon certain legends in the Southern Sperm Whale fisheries, and illustrated by the author's own personal experience, of two years & more, as a harpooner." Although Melville exaggerated his role onboard the *Acushnet* by calling himself a harpooner, he was steadfast in his belief that the book would be very new and appealing: "I do not know that the subject treated of has ever been worked up by a romancer, or indeed, by any writer, in any adequate manner." He was certain the completed book would stand out from anything else yet written, and saw it as both a romantic and realistic tale. Although many critics were beginning to think Melville's best writing days were behind him, one reviewer of *White-Jacket* shared the author's confidence in his own ultimate greatness. "Keep your eye on Herman Melville. If his present field, or rather ocean of literature, should ever become fruitless of pursuit, he will be famous in other fields. There is a humor, and sparkle of rhetoric in his writings, which, if he lives to be the man equal in years to Irving, Cooper and Paulding, will rank him as high on the chalk-notch of fame as they."

TO THE BERKSHIRES

While Melville toiled away on his manuscript, which he referred to as *The Whale*, Maria was finalizing plans for an early summer vacation in Pittsfield. Twelve years had passed since her last visit to the Berkshires, and the chance to reconnect with her sister-in-law Mary Melvill, whose husband Thomas had recently passed away in Galena, Illinois, seemed like a fitting reason to make the long-overdue trip back to the Melvill's farm. Mary was staying at the old estate with her son, Robert, and his wife and children. With mounting bills to pay and improvements to be made, Robert was still running it as a boarding house. He required a steady stream of well-paying and distinguished guests to keep the property afloat. Maria timed her arrival for the beginning of June, aware that the house might be too packed with guests at the height of summer to be comfortable.

Although her stay in the Berkshires was short and she soon moved on to Lansingburgh to reconnect with other relatives, Maria's idea of an excursion to the Berkshires must have resonated with everyone in the New York household. In short order, they all followed suit, abandoning the oppressive heat and congestion of New York City in July for the beauty and simplicity of country life in Pittsfield. Although the exact comings and goings of individual family members are not clear, during the summer of 1850 Augusta, Fanny, Kate, Allan and Sophia, as well as Lizzie, Herman and the children were all in residence at Melvill Place. It was the height of the season, and the Berkshires shone with all its bucolic splendor, providing the perfect setting for a family reunion at a place they all loved so dearly.

The railroad station in Pittsfield as it would have appeared circa 1850.
Courtesy of The Berkshire Historical Society

When they alighted from the train in Pittsfield, the Melvilles could not help but notice that the town had grown and changed greatly since their childhood summer holidays. As a visitor from New Hampshire wrote in an article that appeared in the Portsmouth *Journal* on August 21, 1852, Pittsfield was now "a large and beautiful town," with "beautiful dwellings scattered around; gardens laid out with the most exquisite taste, in which every one seemed to vie with his neighbor for the finest display; and what seemed to me better than all, they were not fenced in so as to be seen only by the privileged few, but low fences and open slatwork enabled the passer by to see and admire."

CHANGES AT MELVILL PLACE

Like the town, Melvill Place was much changed over the last twelve years. The transformation from elegant family estate to summer boarding house had to be jarring, especially for Herman who had cherished his time there so deeply. When he arrived, he was shocked to learn that Robert had just sold the entire property to a wealthy young English merchant named John Rowland Morewood and his American wife Sarah Ann. Until the last few years, the Morewoods had been content at their summer retreat in Carmansville, New York, just north of the city along the Hudson River in what today is known as the Fort Washington area. But the location was losing much of its charm to aggressive urban sprawl and the couple had grown unhappy with their now compromised views, where new buildings and busy railroad tracks marred the landscape. The Berkshires seemed like a paradise in comparison, and Melvill Place rang true to them as the perfect country retreat, though certainly in need of improvements. The house was also a comfortable and easy distance from their main residence in Manhattan. With a final purchase price of just $6,500 agreed upon only weeks before Melville's arrival in Pittsfield, Herman must have been jealous and angry that he did not have the opportunity to purchase the family estate himself.

After dusting off the shock of it, Herman was grateful his own visit would not be disrupted by the Morewoods taking immediate possession of the property, as they had first planned a holiday to England. With spirits somewhat lifted, the family settled in to enjoy themselves. Cousin Robert invited Melville to come along on a several days' long wagon tour of the countryside, inspecting crops and farms as part of Robert's role as the Chairman of the Viewing Committee of the Berkshire Agricultural Society.

Shaker Village in Hancock.

The Shaker Colony at Hancock was a popular destination in the mid 19th century. Tourists and locals visited the village to buy Shaker products and witness their religious fervor.

Courtesy of The Berkshire Athenaeum, Pittsfield, MA

The Hawthornes lived in the "Little Red House" March, 1850 to November, 1851. The house burned in 1890; a replica stands in its place.

Courtesy of The Berkshire Museum

Melville purchased a copy of the 1829 *History of the County of Berkshire, Massachusetts* by Stockbridge resident David Dudley Field to use as a reference guide during the outing, and on the morning of their departure, Melville's Aunt Mary presented him with a copy of Nathaniel Hawthorne's recent short story collection *Mosses from an Old Manse*.

Hawthorne's recent and hugely successful first book, *The Scarlet Letter*, had made him an instant celebrity, though he shunned publicity and was known to be a recluse. Perhaps to keep a lower profile, Hawthorne, his wife Sophia and their two children had recently left Salem for the Berkshires, setting up in a small red cottage overlooking Stockbridge Bowl in nearby Lenox, part of an estate owned by William Aspinwall Tappan. Hawthorne would be in good company by choosing the rolling hills of Western Massachusetts as the backdrop to furthering his creative genius. Other literary greats who had called the Berkshires home over the last few decades included Henry Wadsworth Longfellow, William Cullen Bryant, Catharine Maria Sedgwick, and Oliver Wendell Holmes, who twenty years earlier had written "The Last Leaf," a poem about the late and famous revolutionary war hero Major Thomas Melvill.

A BROAD VIEW

The trip with Robert around the county, though only a few days' long, was important for Melville because it was the first opportunity he had ever had to experience a wide-eyed view of the area as a tourist. Starting out from Pittsfield, the pair headed first to Lenox, then over to Richmond and back to Lenox, where they were put up for the night at Captain Caleb Smith's, a "glorious place, & fine old fellow." They made their way further south, surveying the towns of Stockbridge, admiring Monument Mountain; they continued down through Great Barrington to Egremont, Sheffield and then looped back to Stockbridge, where Herman caught a late train back to the house in Pittsfield. The outing provided an overview of daily life and its rhythms in the Berkshires, and Melville enjoyed it immensely. Animated by his sightseeing tour, he pressed on to experience even more of the county before he needed to return to New York, and made one last outing to the nearby Shaker colony at Hancock.

SUMMER GUESTS

Leaving his family to continue rusticating in Pittsfield, Melville went back to New York the last week of July. He would not remain there very long. No sooner had he unpacked his bags than he set about making his routine stop at Duyckinck's library for a new infusion of books. He was bursting with amusing and engaging descriptions of his one week sojourn in the Berkshires, and to Duyckinck, who had been trapped in the city for far too long, the stories of his friend's vacation in the country were irresistible. Duyckinck and Cornelius Mathews, another writer and editor friend, both readily accepted Melville's hasty invitation to join him back in Pittsfield the following week.

It was a magnificent, if not thoroughly thought out plan. Melville was incredibly indebted to Duyckinck, both for his generosity in bringing him into the literary fold of New York and his lending such a profuse amount of books over the past few years, and this was an opportunity for Melville to return the favor. By playing grand host at the Melvill Place and using it as a base for exploring the charms of the Berkshires, Melville could also be assured of compelling literary discussions with two trusted editors and friends, and perhaps some reassurance and advice as he continued to wrestle with *The Whale*. So caught up in his own reverie about the perfect weekend, Melville hardly checked in with Robert to make sure there was even room at the farm—which there was not. The pair would instead have to take rooms at the Berkshire House in town for the duration of their stay.

The Weekend

On Friday, August 2nd, Duyckinck and Mathews set out for the Berkshires by train. En route, they were delighted to meet David Dudley Field, Jr., the eldest son of the author of the *History of the County of Berkshire, Massachusetts*, which Melville had consulted on his roundabout trip with Robert the previous week. The younger Field was a successful New York lawyer, and as the train rambled along, the men chatted about their professions, their interests and plans for their stays in the country. An energetic and consummate entertainer, Field came up with an idea for the New York literary men to meet "all the celebrities of Stockbridge" at a party at his family home, which could be preceded by a hike up Monument Mountain, made famous by the poet and longtime Berkshire resident William Cullen Bryant. Delighting in the hospitality of a man they had just met, intrigued by his ability to pull together a guest list of literary notables and anxious to take in the scenery on their first visit, Duyckinck and Mathews eagerly accepted his invitation and looked forward to telling Melville of their good fortune.

From the moment they stepped off the train, Duyckinck and Mathews found the countryside to be intoxicating, and Duyckinck soon wrote to his wife of the Berkshires' "pure & bracing mountain air." Sarah Morewood, soon-to-be mistress of the house, was in residence, and immediately took charge of activities for the first-time visitors. Gregarious, with seemingly boundless energy, she first arranged an "afternoon excursion to Pontusac Lake, some seven miles westward."

By all accounts, Duyckinck fell in love with the Berkshires immediately. Captivated by the rolling hills and meadows that stretched out before him, he wrote to his wife extolling the beauty of the landscape:

> The country is a broken plain surrounded by ranges of mountains, of which from the spot where I am looking over the spires of pleasant Pittsfield the cleft two humped Saddleback is the hugest wonder. But I wont describe scenery or tell you of the dark lakes set in the hollows or the murmuring brooks of the meadows, whose cool pebbly sound is only surpassed by the breezes in the tree tops above them. I will tell you nothing of the languishing elms whose foliage swoons in the luxury of air. To tell of these things to a lady encased in hot bricks in New York would be unprovoked cruelty were I not bound to a full and faithful account of my wanderings and did I not hope to make a convert to that beautiful part of the country. I assure you the Poets have made no mistake. The air is balm and a great many other things.

He was equally impressed with the old Melvill Place, "quite a piece of mouldering rural grandeur," that was "a rare place—an old family mansion, wainscoted and stately, with large halls & chimneys." He was impressed with his host's knowledge of the property, and noted "Herman Melville knows every stone & tree & will probably make a book of its features."

A CHAMPAGNE PICNIC ON MONUMENT MOUNTAIN

David Dudley Field, Jr.'s outing to Monument Mountain was arranged for August 5, 1850. That morning, Duyckinck, Mathews and Melville rode

Sarah Morewood was known throughout the Berkshires for her large and lively parties at Broadhall, the Melvill family home that she purchased with her husband Roland in the summer of 1850.

Courtesy of The Berkshire Athenaeum, Pittsfield, MA

Painting of Pontoosuc Lake by Herman Haeussler, 1897
From the collection of The Berkshire Historical Society

THE LAKE PONTOOSUCE
(SELECTED STANZAS)

Crowning a bluff where gleams the lake below,
Some pillared pines in well-spaced order stand
And like an open temple show.
And here in best of seasons bland,
Autumnal noon-tide, I look out
From dusk arcades on sunshine all about.

Beyond the lake, in upland cheer
Fields, pastoral fields, and barns appear,
They skirt the hills where lonely roads
Revealed in links thro' tiers of woods
Wind up to indistinct abodes
And faery-peopled neighborhoods;
While further fainter mountains keep
Hazed in romance impenetrably deep.

Look, corn in stacks, on many a farm,
And orchards ripe in languorous charm,
As dreamy nature, feeling sure
Of all her genial labor done,
And the last mellow fruitage won,
Would idle out her term mature;
Reposing like a thing reclined
In kinship with man's meditative mind.

—by Herman Melville, first published in 1924

A view of Monument Mountain from Edward Hitchcock's *Geology of Massachusetts* (1841).

down from Pittsfield to Stockbridge on the train with Field's fellow invited guest Oliver Wendell Holmes, who had a summer house just east of the Melvill farm. After a short trip along the Housatonic Railroad, the four men arrived in the village of Stockbridge and went to Field's nearby Laurel Cottage on Main Street, to await the rest of the party. To everyone's delight and surprise, the usually reclusive Hawthorne appeared, as well as his Boston publisher, James T. Fields, with his new bride, Eliza. Henry Sedgwick, brother of Stockbridge novelist Catharine Sedgwick and recently hired attorney in his father and Field's New York law practice, as well as Joel T. Headley, the celebrated author of *Napoleon and His Marshals*, were also on the guest list. Field's second wife Harriett and daughter Jeanie rounded out the group. An organizer extraordinaire, within just a few days' time Field had successfully put together an impressive group of seven distinguished literary men, as well as a handful of other notable Berkshirites, for what would prove to be an unforgettable day.

Though the weather looked overcast and inclement at the onset, the assembled party decided to go ahead and make the three-mile carriage ride south from Stockbridge to the base of the mountain. Once they started climbing up the rambling paths, Duyckinck and Hawthorne chatted about *The Scarlet Letter* while other hikers exchanged clever and humorous banter. As one guest recorded later, everyone was "rambling, scrambling, climbing, rhyming—puns flying off in every direction like sparks among the bushes." Before they reached the summit, a swift-moving storm passed overhead, and they took great joy in imagining themselves as passengers on a great sea voyage caught in a squall. Melville pretended to haul in sails while Holmes professed seasickness, and hilarity and general silliness ensued. Once the rain ceased the procession finally reached the top, where they ceremoniously read local poet William Cullen Bryant's "Monument Mountain," an unhappy tale of an Indian princess who is unable to marry her true love, and in her great sorrow throws herself from the rocky cliff at the summit. After the dramatic reading and rounds of applause, the group celebrated with champagne, toasting to "long life to the dear old poet" and then made their way back down the mountain and on to the Field's house for an elaborate supper. After desserts, cigars and brandy, a few ventured further, dashing off to the nearby Ice Glen to explore its dark, cold caves and scramble over its moss-covered, massive piles of rocks. Back at Laurel Cottage, Hawthorne was among the first to depart, anxious to find his way home by carriage before nightfall, while the others chose to remain until the 10 o'clock train back up to Pittsfield. It had been a remarkable day of adventure, laughter and good cheer, but it had also been a day of new bonds and friendships, especially for Melville and Hawthorne.

It is impossible to underestimate the importance of their meeting on this day, and how the resulting friendship that ensued changed both of their lives— and their work—forever. On the hike and during the ensuing activities back at Laurel Cottage, Melville and Hawthorne realized they shared an immediate and important connection, and before the day was out, Hawthorne had already invited Melville and his guests to visit the Red House the next day for further conversation and socializing. Both were in the middle of important writing projects—Melville was hard at work on *The Whale*, while Hawthorne was in the middle of writing stories based on his old seven-gabled house back in Salem. Hawthorne was just enough older to act as a sort of father figure to Melville, and was an excellent listener. His writing style was similar to Melville in that he was determined to write what he wished, rather than bend to what the market dictated. Both men also knew tragedy first hand, as they had each lost their fathers early on in life. Hawthorne shared Melville's deep longing and respect for the sea because both his grandfather and father had been sea captains. Hawthorne's father also suffered from depression and moodiness, not unlike Allan Melvill and, increasingly, Herman himself. The two authors had fallen into an immediate and intense kinship.

In the days following the Monument Mountain outing, Melville quickly read and willingly offered to pen an anonymous review of Hawthorne's *Mosses from an Olde Manse* for an upcoming edition of Duyckinck's *The Literary World* publication. Hastily writing throughout the remainder of his stay, he completed it in time for Duyckinck to carry back to New York. When the review appeared in print shortly thereafter, it was not simply an example of one author praising the work of another, but instead was richly laced with awe and reverence. "A man of deep and noble nature has seized me in this seclusion. His wild witch voice rings through me; or in softer cadences, I seem to hear it in the songs of the hillside birds that sing in the larch trees at my window."

On Monday, August 12th, when Evert Duyckinck and Cornelius Mathews stepped back on the train bound for New York, everyone and everything seemed completely, magically different. During their week-long stay in the Berkshires, major literary figures made new professional

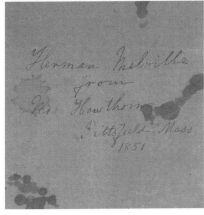

An engraving of Nathaniel Hawthorne that his wife, Sophia, presented to Melville in March 1851.

A note in the hand of Lizzie Melville, attached to the back of the picture, which identifies the provenance of the engraving.

Courtesy of The Berkshire Athenaeum, Pittsfield, MA
Photo by Eric Korenman

connections and forged new friendships, visitors and residents alike explored breathtaking mountaintops and acted as sightseers, even visiting the nearby Shaker settlement. There were long, languid days and lavish evening parties, including a masquerade ball hosted by Sarah Morewood. Though the first to express it, Duyckinck was not the only one who felt utterly transformed. "Ten years of repressed nature in me, suddenly exploding[,] are not to be bottled down again in a hurry."

SYNERGY

The weekend had been a transcendent experience for everyone, and the attraction between Melville and the Hawthornes was mutual from the very beginnings of their acquaintance. Hawthorne's wife, Sophia, wrote to her mother shortly after meeting the famed "Typee," describing in remarkable detail a conversation about the magnetism between the two men.

> He said Mr. Hawthorne was the first person whose physical being appeared to him wholly in harmony with the intellectual and spiritual…He said the sunny air & pensiveness, the symmetry of his face, the depth of his eyes, 'the gleam—the shadow—& the peace supreme all were in exact response to the high calm intellect, the glowing, deep heart—the purity of actual and spiritual life…he found himself talking to Mr. Hawthorne to a great extent. He said Mr. Hawthorne's great but hospitable silence drew him out—that it was astonishing how *sociable* his silence was…He said sometimes they would walk along without talking on either side, but that even then they seemed to be very social.

Shy and reclusive herself, Sophia was still deeply intrigued and impressed by her husband's new friend, and her letter paints an extraordinary portrait of both Melville's physical characteristics as well as his complex personality.

> *Mr.* Melville is a person of great ardor & simplicity. He is all on fire with the subject that interests him. It rings through his frame like a cathedral bell. His truth and honesty shine out at every point…/…a man with a true warm heart & a soul & an intellect,—with life to his fingertips—earnest,

sincere, & reverent, very tender & *modest*...He has very keen perceptive power, but what astonishes me is that his eyes are not large & deep. He seems to see every thing very accurately. How he can do so with his small eyes, I cannot tell. They are not keen eyes, either, but quite undistinguished in any way.

Sophia refers to Melville's poor eyesight, which had plagued him since childhood, likely due to a severe bout of measles. As the years passed, Melville's vision became more and more compromised, to the point when even reading his own handwriting was painful.

His nose is straight & rather handsome, his mouth expressive of sensibility and emotion. He is tall & erect, with an air free, brave & manly. When conversing, he is full of gesture & force, & loses himself in his subject—There is no grace nor polish—once in a while, his animation gives place to a singularly quiet expression out of those eyes, to which I have objected; an indrawn, dim look, but which at the same time makes you feel that he is at that instant taking deepest note of what is before him—It is a strange, lazy glance, but with a power in it quite unique. It does not seem to penetrate through you, but to take you into himself..."

Herman's momentous meeting and ensuing friendship with Nathaniel Hawthorne would prove to be the lynchpin to a new and pivotal chapter in the author's life.

A sketch of Arrowhead done by Herman Melville, circa 1860, which is now lost. The image first appeared in print in one of the earliest biographies of the author by Raymond Weaver entitled *Herman Melville: Mariner and Mystic*.
Image reproduced from Hershel Parker's Herman Melville, A Biography, Volume 2, 1851-1891

7

A House of His Own

At the end of August 1850, Herman, Lizzie, Malcolm and Maria were still in residence at the Melvill farm, and Augusta wrote to a friend that it seemed as if they might not ever leave. "Herman & Lizzie still prolong their rusticating, & are so happy among the mountains of Berkshire, that it seems impossible to tear themselves away." They were content to stay for different reasons—Melville desperately wanted to be in close contact with his new mentor and confidante Hawthorne, and Lizzie looked forward to the opportunity to see her father and stepmother in the first week of September, during one of Shaw's regular visits as a circuit court judge in Lenox. Maria enjoyed being in the company of her extended family, and all of them preferred the country to city living, especially in the summertime. The reality of having lost the family home to the Morewoods, though they would prove to be good friends and caretakers of the beloved property, was another important reason why Melville had a difficult time relinquishing his time in the Berkshires. He had come to the conclusion that it was nearly impossible to imagine leaving the landscape and the people he held so dearly, and in his own mind, it was inevitable that he would remain there.

On September 14, 1850 Melville surprised his family and friends by purchasing the farm of Dr. John Brewster, which was adjacent to the eastern portion of the old Melvill property and near the Oliver Wendell Holmes estate. By all accounts, it was an impulsive purchase. The farm had not been advertised in Pittsfield's *Sun* newspaper, and Melville did not pursue other real estate possibilities or haggle over the price with Brewster— an astonishing $6,500 for a "large quaint old house" with 160 acres of

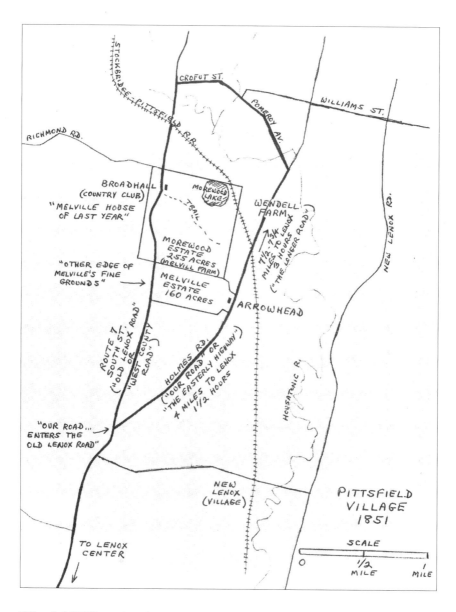

"Pittsfield Village, 1851" a manuscript map by Stockbridge resident
Lion Miles, 1997.
Courtesy Lion Miles

farmland and woods. Even though the house afforded a spectacular view of Mount Greylock and the surrounding countryside, the sum Melville was willing to pay was exorbitant, especially considering the Morewoods paid the same amount for a much grander and well-known house, nearly 300 acres including a lake, and various outbuildings. Melville could ill afford the purchase, especially given the poor sales of his recent

As Augusta explained in a letter to her friend Mary Blatchford, "What think you of the name of our place—Arrow-head. It is so called from the number of these Indian relics which have been found."

books and his gradually waning reputation among the reading public.

To afford the down payment, Melville appealed to his father-in-law Lemuel Shaw, who appreciated the virtues of Berkshire living during his own regular visits to Lenox. Shaw may have also been swayed to help finance Melville because a house in Pittsfield was far closer than one in New York, and thus Shaw could be assured of seeing his daughter and new grandson there regularly. Shaw agreed to loan Melville $3,000 against Lizzie's inheritance for the down payment. Additionally, Melville took out a mortgage from Brewster for $1,500, promising to pay $90 per year in interest on the loan. He had every confidence his budding writing career would provide an income that would make major improvements at his new home possible in the near future.

Though Melville was resolute, his friends and family were surprised by such a bold, impulsive and extravagant purchase. Deep in his heart, Melville was convinced there was no way he could possibly tear himself away from Hawthorne or the Berkshires. In his mind, the property was perfect. It was directly adjacent to the old Melville farm, was just an easy six miles north of Hawthorne's Red House in Lenox, and the dramatic and majestic views of Mount Greylock were particularly good from what would become his second floor study. When seated at his desk, the view of the mountain's "camelback" silhouette would be an inspiration and constant reminder of the great white whale at the center of what the thirty-one year old increasingly argued would be his most ambitious and important work yet.

Ebullient, just one day after the sale Melville harnessed a horse and rode down to Lenox to announce his news to the Hawthornes. "He drove up one

'Melville's Residence,' woodcut by W. Roberts, from *Cyclopedia of American Literature*, by Evert A. Duyckinck and George L. Duyckinck (New York, 1855)
Courtesy of The Berkshire Athenaeum, Pittsfield, MA

superb moonlight night & said he had bought an estate six miles from us, where he is really going to build a real towered house—an actual tower…So we shall have him for a neighbour," Sophia Hawthorne recalled. Her letter reveals that Melville's intention was to tear down the rustic farmhouse to build a larger, fashionable house with a writing tower where he could survey the mountain ranges and valleys, and feel himself to be on top of the world in his writing and his career.

Though Allan, Sophia and for the time being Kate, would all stay behind in New York, the rest of the Melvilles—Maria, Helen, Augusta and Fanny planned to join Herman and Lizzie in Pittsfield, making the farmhouse their primary residence. Helen and Fanny took advantage of the last few days in New York to scour the fabric district, shopping for elegant silks, satins and velvets for window draperies and upholstery, while in a flurry of activity, other family members and servants eagerly packed up household belongings.

News both of Morewood's purchase of the old family farm and Melville's own real estate transaction reached the reading public in the Berkshires on October 17th. The *Sun* reported that "Melvill Farm, one mile south of the village" had recently been purchased by John Morewood, and was "undergoing extensive repairs" while Morewood was in Europe. The article continued, explaining that Herman Melville had purchased "a portion of the Farm formerly owned by the late Mr. David Bush, a short distance south of the summer residence of Dr. Oliver Wendell Holmes, and contemplates the erection, at no distant day, as we understand, of 'a house to suit him" in a beautiful grove on the premises. The situation he has purchased commands one of the most extensive and splendid views in Berkshire."

SETTING UP HOUSEKEEPING AT ARROWHEAD

Captain David Bush, one of Pittsfield's early settlers, had built the Melvilles' newly acquired clapboard farmhouse in the 1780s. Bush was the first town clerk, and in addition to farming his land, he likely operated a modest tavern and small inn. The property remained in the Bush family until Brewster purchased it in 1844; six years later Melville took ownership. Melville named the property Arrowhead. As Augusta explained in a letter to her friend Mary Blatchford, "What think you of the name of our place— Arrow-head. It is so called from the number of these Indian relics which have been found."

Thrilled to finally be a full-time Berkshire resident, Melville kept occupied during his early weeks and months at Arrowhead with domestic duties—in a letter to Duyckinck, he explained, "Until today, I have been as busy as man could be. Everything to be done, & scarcely anyone to help me do it. But I trust that before a great while we shall be all 'to rights,' and I shall take my ease on mine mountain. For a month to come, tho', I expect to be in the open air all day, except when assisting in lifting a bedstead or a bureau."

Outdoor chores—such as harvesting apples or other crops, splitting wood, milking and feeding cows, or tending to the horse—kept Melville delightfully happy. Because he forbade the women to drive the wagon themselves, he was regularly called into duty as a chauffeur each time one of them wanted to go into town, attend church services at the nearby St. Stephen's Episcopalian Church, or head off to visit cousins who were still living at the Melvill Farm before the Morewoods took full possession. Between farm chores, setting up housekeeping and seeing to his family responsibilities, Melville often had a difficult time carving out enough time for writing during his first fall at Arrowhead, but at the conclusion of each day, whether pleasantly fatigued from his efforts in the fields or at his desk, he waxed poetic about his good fortune and the sublime scenery surrounding him.

> It has been a most glowing & Byzantine day—the heavens reflecting the tints of the October apples in the orchard—nay, the heavens themselves looking so ripe & ruddy, that it must be harvest-home with the angels, & Charles' Wain be heaped high as Saddle-back with Autumn's sheaves.—You should see the maples—you should see the young perennial pines—the red blazings of the one contrasting with the painted green of the other, and the wide flushings of the autumn air harmonizing both. I tell you that sunrises and sunsets grow side by side in these woods, & momentarily moult in the falling leaves.

Other family members were equally overjoyed by the move to the Berkshires. By mid October, Augusta extolled the benefits of country life:

> It far surpasses my expectations. The scenery is magnificent. I could never have imagined anything more beautiful—more varied—in every direction, it stretches away in mountain,

hill & valley, all glowing with gorgeous tints of autumn. I have no doubt we see it now under its most beautiful aspect, for I hardly think the fresh green of June can be as well suited to its wild sublimity…I wish you were by my side this moment, dear Mary, to watch the changing light and shade upon the forest slope just before me—it is exquisite—The glowing scarlet of the maples contrast so brightly with the more subdued tints of their woodland sisters, & all wrapt in that soft dreamy haze which characterizes a mountain sunset…—I declare it has made even prosaic me, poetical— what then would be its effect on you.—I really believe that I could at this moment indite a sonnet.

While the location and views the house afforded were ideal, family members did acknowledge that the simple layout of the house around a central chimney had its limitations. Augusta explained that "Our old farm house cannot boast much in point of beauty, but it is delightfully comfortable & that is all that is really necessary in the country. It is an old house, counting its seventy years or more, & though outwardly modernized, retains all its ancient appearance within. It is built after that peculiarly quaint style of architecture which places the chimney—the hugest in proportions—immediately in the centre, & the rooms around it. An arrangement so totally void of grace & beauty, must surely possess some counterbalancing advantage, but as yet I have been unable to discover it…" She was particularly charmed by a simple corner cupboard in the parlor, playfully boasting it as the "gem of the collection," and explaining that "(w)e have left it standing for its oddity, but elevate it from its ignoble use into doing duty as an 'etage[re]'."

A DAILY ROUTINE

By November, Herman, Lizzie, Maria, Helen, Augusta, Kate and Fanny all felt settled in at their new home. When Lizzie decided to take their son Malcolm to Boston for an extended visit with her family for the Thanksgiving holiday, Melville finally felt he could put aside the flurry of domestic concerns that had preoccupied him for so long, and give his full attention to finish edits and revisions to the manuscript for *The Whale*. Penning a letter to Duyckinck, who was understandably interested to know how the book was coming along, Melville described the typical arc of his day at Arrowhead.

Do you want to know how I pass my time?—I rise at eight—thereabouts—& go to my barn—say good-morning to the horse, & give him his breakfast. (It goes to my heart to give him a cold one, but it can't be helped) Then, pay a visit to my cow—cut up a pumpkin or two for her, & stand by to see her eat it—for it's a pleasant sight to see a cow move her jaws—she does it so mildly & with such a sanctity.—My own breakfast over, I go to my work-room & light my fire—then spread my M.S.S. on the table—take one business squint at it, & fall to with a will. At 2 ½ P.M. I hear a preconcerted knock at my door, which (by request) continues till I rise & go to the door, which serves to wean me effectively from my writing, however interested I may be…My evenings I spent in a sort of mesmeric state in my room—not being able to read—only now & then skimming over some large-printed book.

During the winter months of 1851, Melville regularly squirreled himself away in the upstairs study, furiously wrestling with the white whale on page after page. Gazing out the window to a snow-covered landscape in an almost hypnotic state, he often felt like he was looking "out of a port-hole of a ship in the Atlantic," and the overall effect was "a sort of sea-feeling here in the country." So as not to disturb his creative process, a household servant was under strict instructions to leave his lunch at the door of the study, to take or not as he wished. One chapter after another, Melville surrendered his barely legible text to his sister Augusta or Helen for clear copying, and then returned to his desk for another round until late in the afternoon. As each day exhaustingly came to a close, he hitched up the horses to a sleigh wagon for an exhilarating ride into town to stop by the post office or to visit his cousins. Craving fresh air to clear his mind and lighten his spirits, these daily outings were imperative both for his physical and mental well being.

HOUSEHOLD IMPROVEMENTS

Melville's original plan was to use the farmhouse as a temporary residence until he had the opportunity to build a larger, more modern and impressive house with a writing tower, set back from the road and properly and grandly landscaped. But in February 1851, six months following the move, the

Fourth Avenue brownstone remained unsold, a troubling fact especially because Melville still owed John Brewster the considerable balance due on his mortgage, and still had unpaid household bills to settle. The chances of being able to afford a completely new house were looking very unlikely, and the reality was beginning to set in that he needed to rethink how he could make the present farmhouse suit his needs and his ambition.

As the harsh effects of winter set in, the house had begun to look considerably less charming than it had during the height of summer. On the exterior, several outbuildings needed repair and the barns badly needed to be painted. On the interior, not only did the parlor walls need fresh paper and paint, but much of the upholstered furniture brought up from New York had the appearance of being tired and worn. With so many family members and at least one servant in residence, it was also crowded, especially by modern standards. At the back of the house, the Irish cook and servant, both called Mary, worked in a rather primitive and small detached kitchen, without a sink, drain or pump. The house was not up to the standards they required, and unless improvements were made soon, the Melvilles would have a difficult time hosting the guests they anticipated during the approaching summer season.

Having no money to build a new house, nor to pay Brewster, Melville resigned himself to make improvements to the present house and barns. In March, he hired men to begin work on a narrow porch to be built along the northeast corner of the house, directly below his study window. The piazza, as he called it, would share the same magnificent view of "Saddleback" as the upstairs study, but would be strictly intended for Melville's own musings and guests. It was designed to be small, accommodating just a few chairs. Thinking more practically, he also ordered the workmen to lay foundations for a new kitchen and wood-house at the back of the house. Whether or not the renovations were necessary, it was a strange and expensive time of year to begin outside work, especially considering that the hired men would need to work harder and longer hours, ultimately at added expense, to dig through the frozen ground.

With the work underway, Melville was relieved when a purchaser came forward for the Fourth Avenue house in New York. The sale closed in at $7,000, but there was still a hefty mortgage to pay Brewster, as well as fees on the transaction and unpaid mortgage payments to settle up, and the barely touched piles of household bills. In preparation for spring planting, Melville had also to begin purchasing garden seeds and cuttings, and he owed his publisher Harper & Brothers $700 for outstanding expenses related to *White-Jacket*. Envisioning a proper life in the country, Maria was advocating even further expenditures. While visiting Allan and Sophia in New York, she priced "oak paper" for the parlor and expressed the need for a manservant back at Arrowhead, as "you cannot do without one & this is the place to procure one." When Melville realized it would be impossible to pay back Brewster in full, pay for renovations and still have cash available for regular household expenditures, he quickly and very discreetly took out yet another loan, this time from an old Lansingburgh friend, T.D. Stewart for $2,050 at 9% interest.

THE FIRST FULL SUMMER IN RESIDENCE

With Hawthorne's guiding faith and inspiration in his work, Melville wrapped up the final details of his manuscript about the great white whale and delivered it to Harper & Brothers by July. While his London publisher would keep his original title for the book, *The Whale*, Harper & Brothers entitled the American edition *Moby-Dick*.

Exhausted from the writing process and unable to afford much help on the farm, Melville gladly surrendered himself to the seemingly more mundane work of a farmer, plowing his fields, planting his crops and attending to various carpentry jobs on the house and barns. He looked forward to a summer respite from his writing, which had become all-consuming the previous winter, and relished the opportunity to once again entertain and play the gracious host to his literary friends and extended family. Though Arrowhead was a humbler property than he had envisioned, Melville still established himself as a noted author living the country life in the Berkshires, a neighbor and friend to other literary notables like Hawthorne, Oliver Wendell Holmes and Catharine Sedgwick.

July and August saw many guests coming and going at Arrowhead— Allan, Sophia and their daughters, various members of the Shaw family, a second visit for Evert Duyckinck accompanied by his brother, George, and other Melvill cousins and distant relatives. Finally in full residence at the old Melvill Place, now named Broadhall, Sarah Morewood distinguished herself in the community as an extraordinary hostess, arranging large, elaborate masked balls, tea parties and outings for friends and guests. The Boston *Evening Transcript* described Broadhall as "the very home of "free-hearted hospitality," and described Sarah's "real talent which she so preeminently possesses of putting her guests at ease."

The Duyckinck brothers were very content at Arrowhead and thrilled to be in the Berkshires, their accommodations "simple and excellent with country nature and city taste." In extolling the beauty of the landscape, Evert exclaimed, "You must have a peep at this region to believe the lightness and purity of the air, the fragrant coolness and the blue and purple distances in which it is set. The grounds would satisfy an English nobleman—for the noble maples and elms and the various wooded seclusions and outlooks and all for the price of a bricked in city enclosure of 25 x 100!"

With a full roster of activities, such as picnics, hikes, walks, visits to have dinners with Hawthorne "in fine Spanish al fresco style" or excursions to nearby New Lebanon to see the Shakers, the Melvilles and their guests were firmly at the center of a social whirl of summer in the Berkshires. A crowning "grand excursion of the week to Saddleback, Williamstown &c, by railway &c" organized by Sarah Morewood for the Duyckincks, Melvilles and other guests kept everyone completely and thrillingly entertained, exactly as Melville had wished.

A photograph of Melville's children, Stanwix, Frances, Malcolm and
Elizabeth, circa 1860.
Courtesy of The Berkshire Athenaeum, Pittsfield, MA

8

YEARS AT ARROWHEAD

B etween the years of 1851 and 1855, Melville's three youngest children Stanwix (Stannie), Elizabeth (Bessie) and Frances (Fanny) were born at Arrowhead. It was a full house, with a cook, a maid and an occasional farm hand also in residence, and few quiet places to find a retreat from the constant din of family life. Fortunately, Herman's sisters—Helen, Augusta and Fanny—as well as Maria and Lizzie often traveled, visiting friends and family in Boston, New York and in the upstate town of Gansevoort, where Maria still had relatives. Despite the commotion, Melville stuck to his writing with rigor and discipline, shutting himself in his study and pressing on.

MOBY-DICK IN PRINT

Moby-Dick was in print by the fall of 1851 in New York, and Melville hoped for a glowing reception both stateside and abroad. Having dedicated the book to Hawthorne, he surprised his mentor with an elegant presentation copy of the book in October, at a supper in the dining room of the Curtis Hotel in Lenox. Hawthorne was deeply moved by Melville's dedication, and the two men ate, drank, gossiped and lingered before they bid their final farewells to each other. The meeting was bittersweet because it would be the last time the authors would be together in the Berkshires. Hawthorne had suddenly decided to return to Concord, partially due to his dislike of the Berkshires' harsh winters, but also because of a minor dispute with the Tappan family regarding the Red House. Much of Melville's joy in living in the Berkshires came from Hawthorne's proximity; his departure would have a lasting and deep impact. Melville felt overwhelmingly indebted to

MOBY-DICK;

OR,

THE WHALE.

BY

HERMAN MELVILLE,

AUTHOR OF

"TYPEE," "OMOO," "REDBURN," "MARDI," "WHITE-JACKET."

NEW YORK:

HARPER & BROTHERS, PUBLISHERS.

LONDON: RICHARD BENTLEY.

1851.

Title page of the first American edition of *Moby-Dick*.
Courtesy The Berkshire Historical Society

Hawthorne for his friendship and guidance, and Hawthorne's impending departure initiated for Herman the beginnings of an inner turmoil; he questioned his ability to stay the course in his writing and his spirits without his confidante nearby.

Copies of *Moby-Dick* went on sale in the Pittsfield bookstore of Phineas Allen by December 18th. While a few American reviewers had modest praise for it as "a complete exhibition of the art and mystery of whaleology, with graphic pictures of the life and times of whalemen," others misunderstood it and were offended by its seemingly blasphemous approach to religion. A reviewer from the *New York Independent* harshly warned "the Judgment day will hold [Melville] liable for not turning his talents to better account... The book-maker and the book-publisher [Harper's] had better do their work with a view to the trial it must undergo at the bar of God." Such disparaging reviews hindered sales dramatically. In the first two weeks of the American publication, 1,535 copies were sold; over the next two months only 471 sold, and a further decline ensued. The American public largely ignored *Moby-Dick*, having lost interest in their former beloved "Typee." In their eyes, he had essentially "jumped ship" from being an adventure writer and instead become an obtuse, long-winded and scandalous writer of dense narratives laced with far too many lofty references and minutiae.

The London version, *The Whale*, also fared poorly in large part due to publishers who heavily and clumsily edited sections that seemed offensive, and in their edition somehow forgot to include the book's epilogue. In omitting this, they essentially printed the book without its final chapters. Readers were confused and annoyed by the apparent demise of the narrator Ishmael, though in truth his character should have reappeared at the end of the story. While generally speaking Melville's writing found more favor with English readers than with Americans, on both continents readers were increasingly frustrated when he did not stick to the travel and adventure

> "This constant working of the brain, & excitement of the imagination, is wearing Herman out, & you will my dear Peter be doing him a lasting benefit if by your added exersions [sic] you can procure for him a foreign consulship."
> —Maria Melville

narratives that had marked his career's beginnings. "What I feel most moved to write, that is banned—it will not pay," he lamented to Hawthorne. "Yet, altogether, write the *other* way I cannot."

A DOWNWARD SPIRAL

No sooner had he finished *Moby-Dick* and summer guests had departed from Arrowhead, than Melville was at work on another ambitious book, a psychological thriller centered on a romance and complex family relationships, including some scandalous references to incest. Melville's growing obsession with writing—indeed his fury to get his words from his pen to paper—concerned his family, and one of them confessed to Sarah Morewood that he was "now so engaged in a new work as frequently not to leave his room till quite dark in the evening—when he for the first time during the whole day partakes in solid food." The family was worried, as Sarah explained in a letter to George Duyckinck, that "he must therefore write under a state of morbid excitement which will soon injure his health." In New York, others had largely come to an even more blunt conclusion: "The recluse life he was leading made his city friends think that he was slightly insane—he replied that long ago he came to the same conclusion himself."

Written in just a few months, the novel *Pierre* was met with great skepticism by Melville's publishers. With the public's declining interest in his authorship, the growing pile of poor reviews, and no assurances the author would ever give them what they wanted, Harper & Brothers offered a pittance of a contract, and refused to forward Melville money in advance of sales. When his old friend and editor Evert Duyckinck realized that he was the target of a satirical portrait in Melville's new book, he too denounced it publically, and their friendship was badly damaged. Critics were unanimous in their condemnations of both the book and the author himself. The *Southern Quarterly Review* argued there was "no knowing when madness will break out, or in whom," and described the author as having "gone 'clean daft'" in this latest novel. A headline in the *New York Day Book* went so far as to proclaim in a headline simply: "HERMAN MELVILLE CRAZY."

With his writing career spiraling downward at an increasingly alarming pace, life at Arrowhead had turned equally unpleasant. Without an income from his books, Melville was forced to rely on infusions of cash from his father-in-law, and still found himself plunging deeper into debt. The situation caused Melville to be constantly irritated with those around him, especially his wife and children, and he vacillated between furious outbursts and bouts of depression. Even the Shaws, who had shown such faith and generosity towards their author son-in-law, were beginning to worry about Lizzie's well being with him in the household. His questioned sanity and the damage of his devastating reviews were beginning to have an effect on both the Melville and Shaw families' respectability.

Not surprisingly, Melville had also repeatedly defaulted on loan payments to both T.D. Stewart—a loan that Lizzie knew nothing about—as well as the mortgage payments to Brewster. On their own, family members saw Melville's writing career as only bringing an emotional and financial toll, and advocated that he give it up entirely, to find a steadier job that could afford him the travel that he cherished so as a younger man adventuring in the South Pacific. A job as a foreign consulate seemed within reach, especially given the Gansevoort, Melvill and Shaw political connections. Additionally, Hawthorne had been recently named United States Consul in Liverpool, and a position in the foreign service may have been attractive to Melville largely for the reason that he might reconnect with his beloved mentor. Maria was particularly strong in advocating for a career shift, writing to her brother Peter to ask for assistance and warning that "(t)his constant working of the brain, & excitement of the imagination, is wearing Herman out, & you will my dear Peter be doing him a lasting benefit if by your added exersions [sic] you can procure for him a foreign consulship." Not only were those efforts unsuccessful, but Melville suffered another blow when a large fire at Harper & Brothers in New York destroyed many unsold books and printed sheets, and his publishers would need to recoup their huge losses before they would share any

> Reviewers argued in their assessments that though "Hawthorne is more dry, prosaic and detailed, Irving more elegant, careful and popular," Melville was "a kind of wizard; he writes strange and mysterious things that belong to other worlds beyond this tame and everyday place we live in."

The passport Melville used when Lemuel Shaw sent his son-in-law on a solo Grand Tour of Europe. Note that Melville's identifying characteristics were written in his own hand.

From the Herman Melville Collection at The Berkshire Athenaeum

new profits—if there were any—with their author.

Without another career on the horizon, Melville isolated himself, but kept at his writing as if it were in fact a lifeline to his sanity. At a furious pace, he churned out another (now lost) manuscript entitled *Isle of the Cross*, but could not find a publisher to accept it. He then turned to writing short stories, which were moderately successful, though not moneymaking ventures. Between 1853 and 1855 nearly every story he wrote was accepted for serialized publications in either *Putnam's Monthly Magazine* or *Harper's New Monthly Magazine*. Many were soon published as collections in book form. *Israel Potter: His Fifty Years in Exile* and *The Piazza Tales* included "Bartleby, The Scrivener," today considered one of the best American short stories of all time. Many stories were either set at Arrowhead or other locations in the Berkshires, such as the well known "I and My Chimney, " in which the large central chimney of the farmhouse at Arrowhead serves as the chief character in a sketch about domestic life.

Dix & Edwards, publishers of *The Piazza Tales*, marketed the book as ideal summer reading, and placed advertisements in newspapers indicating "For a companion under the broad branches of an old elm in the hot Summer days, keeping company with us to the very borders of dream-land, and soothing the sense into repose, as with the sightings of distant music, we recommend these 'Piazza Tales.'" Even reviewers who had treated Melville so harshly for his last two books argued in their assessments that though "Hawthorne is more dry, prosaic and detailed, Irving more elegant, careful and popular," Melville was "a kind of wizard; he writes strange and mysterious things that belong to other worlds beyond this tame and everyday place we live in." Though these favorable reviews must have been a relief to the beaten-down writer, no one but those closest to him knew that they had come too late, and his own willingness to persevere as a full-time author was fading fast.

By the spring of 1856, the once athletic and handsome sailor had become a reclusive, irascible and despondent man, who had declined physically as well as mentally, suffering in addition to the poor eyesight that had plagued him from childhood, rheumatism and painful sciatica. He began drinking to alleviate his ailments. Layered on top of these problems, he also had loans to T.D. Stewart yet unpaid. With the May 1st date to collect the entire principal looming, Stewart threatened to seize the entire property or force its sale for repayment. Feeling cornered, Melville finally confessed the outstanding loans to Lizzie. Unwilling to give up his beloved Arrowhead in full, together they determined to put a portion of the acreage up for sale.

For Sale by Owner

Appearing in the Sun on April 14th, the advertisement offered "PART of the FARM now occupied by the subscriber, being 80 acres, more than half well wooded, within a mile and a half of Pittsfield village by the County road." Just a month later, the entire property was put up for sale, including the farmhouse, and Melville secured a real estate broker from New York City to assist in finding a New Yorker who might be interested in the property, whether looking to acquire or build a summer house in the Berkshires.

It would have been hard to believe just a few years earlier, but Melville was willing to leave the place that had nurtured and sustained him for so long. In a long letter to Shaw, he admitted, "Lizzie & I have concluded that it may be best for us to remove into some suitable house in the village, that is, if the whole farm can be advantageously sold." Augusta explained that her brother "was convinced that a residence in the country was not the thing for him, & could he have met with an opportunity of disposing of his place he would have done so." By late June, an advertisement in the *Berkshire County Eagle* offered for sale the "place now occupied by the subscriber (two miles and a half from Pittsfield village by the east road to Lenox,) being about seventy acres, embracing meadow, pasture, wood, and orchard, with a roomy and comfortable house. For situation and prospect, this place is among the pleasantest in Berkshire, and has other natural advantages desirable in a country residence."

The house remained unsold, but in July 1856 Melville found a buyer for half of the acreage at Arrowhead—some 80 acres—that fronted the County road. Colonel George S. Willis paid $5,500 for it, a windfall given Melville's financial circumstances. The hitch was that the price could not be paid out directly, but through a complicated set of mortgages and interventions from Judge Shaw, both Brewster and T.D. Stewart were paid off. Melville then signed the deed to Arrowhead over to Shaw, who in turn gave it to Lizzie as part of her inheritance. Shaw had long ago realized that his daughter's own fortune would need to buoy her husband and their family's lifestyle; by essentially gifting the property to her, Shaw single-handedly protected Arrowhead from being sold.

For the time being, Melville's large debts were paid off, and Lizzie owned the remainder of the Arrowhead property outright.

Though the situation looked better, income to cover household bills was still just trickling in, and Melville remained restless and depressed. With the family's support, Shaw offered to send his broken son-in-law on a solo Grand Tour of Europe. Such a trip would give both Lizzie and Herman distance from each other at a time in their marriage when things had become difficult, and the seven-month trip to Scotland, England, the eastern Mediterranean, Italy, Switzerland, Holland and back to England would be therapeutic for Melville on every level. The family also hoped these travels might inspire him to pen another tale of adventure, though Melville made no such promises. When he returned in April 1857 to learn that his most recent book, *The Confidence Man*, had not earned a single penny in income either in the United States or England, he had absolutely no intention of pursuing yet another writing project that would prove fruitless.

While Melville was making his way through Europe, other family members had also left Arrowhead. Herman's sisters Helen and Kate were now married and building lives and families of their own, while Maria, Fanny, and Augusta had set up their own housekeeping at Mansion House, the home of Maria's recently widowed brother Herman Gansevoort, which was located some ten miles north of Saratoga Springs, New York. While they would return to Arrowhead occasionally, the Mansion House was increasingly becoming the new family gathering place. Set among the Adirondack Mountains, it provided a retreat that rivaled what Arrowhead had once been for the family. Lizzie chose to spend her winter with the children in Boston for an extended stay with the Shaws. In April, her brother Lemuel explained that, "Elizabeth has now gone to Pittsfield to set her house in readiness to receive her husband whom she expects sometime in May." Despite all the mental and financial anguish he had put her through for the past several years, Lizzie was still eager to give Herman a proper homecoming at Arrowhead—and she had also vowed to stand by him and try to make things right for the family back at their beloved home in the Berkshires.

Melville returned to Arrowhead with a renewed interest in selling the property. Travel abroad might have reminded him of the opportunities outside Berkshire County, and he may have been attracted to city living as a much-needed change of scenery. Being back at Arrowhead could also have brought back too many painful pangs of nostalgia about Hawthorne. Within just a few weeks, he placed a running advertisement in the *Berkshire County Eagle* describing the property to potential buyers. But the sale generated little interest, and Melville found himself passing another summer in the Berkshires, largely ignoring his writing and instead taking some comfort in his old roles as farmer and caretaker. Without a buyer in sight, however, Melville was not yet in any position to decamp and begin anew in New York as he had hoped. He still needed to find a job that would provide some income.

THE LECTURE CIRCUIT

Without much drive to renew his short story writing, Melville turned his attention to another profession that might take advantage of his former reputation as a gifted storyteller and his recent travels through Europe. A large-scale lecture tour could achieve many things—get him out of the house, especially during the winter months when it felt most confining both mentally and physically, appeal to his restless nature as the lectures would provide speaking engagements throughout the country, and also put him out in front of audiences to be rediscovered. All could be done at a good profit, especially if he was engaging and audiences flocked to hear him speak.

Beginning in the fall of 1857, Melville set out, expounding upon topics such as "Statues in Rome," "Travel: Its Pleasures, Pains and Profits," and "The South Seas." The expectation was for crowds to fill halls, a large swath of the population coming out to see their "Typee" after so many years. They may have imagined him to be more like the handsome rogue traveler from *Typee* and *Omoo*, and most were discouraged to discover instead a frail man facing them on the lectern, inaudible and stiff, who as one reviewer described, could not "for one minute take his eyes from his manuscript." Even though Melville would keep at lecturing on and off through early 1860, strong audiences never materialized, nor did any substantive profit that would make a calculable difference to the family's income.

POETRY

In 1860, as the United States was moving quickly towards Civil War, Melville was largely holed up at Arrowhead, isolating himself in his study. He began to read and write poetry, a secret he shared only with Lizzie. While other members of the family had encouraged Melville to stop writing entirely, Lizzie's faith in his talent had always remained constant, and she was supportive of the poetry as another means for Herman to feed his soul.

Though it gave him solace, outwardly Melville still remained ill and depressed, and when a chance to take a voyage to China with his brother Tom emerged, Lizzie and the rest of the family encouraged him to go, even though the trip would last a full year. Tom had become the captain of the clipper ship *Meteor*, and Melville anticipated that the adventure of being back at sea would be a way to start anew. In his absence, he asked Lizzie's help in arranging for the publication of a volume of his poetry that he had since completed. Wishing to be anonymous and mocking his earlier success, he requested that she abstain from including an inscription, especially one that would read "By the author of Typee, Piddledee, &c." He had written the poetry for his own satisfaction, and while he wanted it to be published and reviewed, he did not want his name associated with it, lest it might tarnish the book's reception. When he docked in San Francisco some months later, Melville had every expectation of finding a volume of poems published and waiting for him at a local bookseller, but to his surprise, publishing houses had rejected the volume.

> "...poetry is a comparatively uncalled-for article in the publishing market—I suppose that if John Milton were to offer 'Paradise Lost' to the Harper's tomorrow, it would be promptly rejected as 'unsuitable' not to say, denounced as dull."
>
> —Lizzie Melville

Ever supportive of her belief in her husband, Lizzie reacted to publishers' rejections with surprising spunk. Writing to Duyckinck, she wrote scathingly that "[I] do not consider its rejection by the publishers as any test of its merit in a literary point of view—well knowing...that *poetry* is a comparatively uncalled-for article in the publishing market—I suppose that if John Milton were to offer 'Paradise Lost' to the Harper's tomorrow, it would be promptly rejected as 'unsuitable' not to say, denounced as dull."

Feeling totally and utterly dejected, Melville hastily cut his trip short, and returned home to Arrowhead from San Francisco.

FADING INTEREST IN THE BERKSHIRES

Weary and depressed, Melville was back in the Berkshires in November 1860, a few days ahead of Lizzie and the children, who were once again in Boston visiting the Shaws. Sarah Morewood offered to put up the Melvilles at Broadhall until Arrowhead could be properly opened up, and Herman eagerly accepted her kind invitation, knowing that by day he would be busy readying his house, "putting up the stoves, airing the bedding—warming the house, and getting up a grand domestic banquet." Lizzie was delighted by Herman's willingness to turn the tables, remembering when she had opened and prepared the house for his arrival from Europe three years earlier. "You see the order of things is completely reversed, since Herman is going on to Pittsfield to get the house ready for *me*—that is, to get Mr. Clark to put the stoves up, and get it *warm* for me to go to work in—A new proverb should be added 'Wives propose—husbands dispose'—don't you think so?" she wrote to Sarah Morewood. Melville's apparent joy at being back in the Berkshires was refreshing. Lizzie wished for a good winter at the house, especially as the extended family continued to worry about the ill effects on his health when in residence there. As Lemuel Shaw wrote to Allan, "I am as deeply impressed as you possibly can be of the necessity of Herman's getting away from Pitts [sic]. He is there solitary, without society, without exercise or occupation except that which is very likely to be injurious to him in over-straining his mind."

While the family continued to try to pursue diplomatic posts for Herman that would get him far away from the Berkshires, work on the farm needed to continue, but in his frailty Melville was unable to do much on his own. Farm hands were in short supply, as many young men had joined the Union army. The property began to show effects of benign neglect, but Melville did what he could, with the help of his children and a handful of servants. Though weakened, he still stuck to his habit of driving into town to get the mail each day, where he could hear the latest telegraph dispatches about the war, and on good days, still ventured out on long rambling walks and hikes. In the seclusion of his study, he continued to write poetry.

Lizzie's father Lemuel Shaw died at age eighty in Boston on March 30, 1861, leaving a large gap in the family and a sizeable fortune to his children, of which Lizzie inherited a total of some $15,000. It was a very handsome sum, especially considering she already owned Arrowhead outright. The fortune, which would certainly make life more comfortable for the Melvilles, afforded them the opportunity to rent a modest but gracious house on East Eighteenth Street in New York for much of the winter. Over the years, they had grown tired of the long and harsh winters in the Berkshires, and the change of scenery and pace in New York City was appealing to them.

Once settled in New York, Herman continued to spend hours each day reading and writing poetry, and also set out on book-buying expeditions in the Broadway-Bowery area of Astor Place, not far from his former house on Fourth Avenue. With Lizzie's fortune secure, although not yet fully realized, he began to pursue other aesthetic interests, especially friendships with fellow intellects such as writer, critic and essayist Henry Tuckerman. With Tuckerman's guidance and his own careful study, Melville began to develop a good eye for painting and engravings, and set about building a significant collection for himself.

> "We passed through some of the wildest and most enchanting scenery, both mountain and valley and I cannot sufficiently congratulate myself that I have seen it before leaving Berkshire."
>
> —Lizzie Melville on the trip she and Herman took before leaving the Berkshires

Returning to Arrowhead in late spring, Herman, Lizzie and the children all reestablished themselves at Arrowhead. The family advertised for a "woman to do the cooking and house-work in a small family, two miles and a half from Pittsfield village. No dairy-work required. To a competent person the HIGHEST wages will be given." Melville also purchased a horse and looked for help on the farm. But as the months wore on, he felt more urgently that he was no longer interested in remaining at Arrowhead. The delight in country living had waned, and the property was once again advertised for sale in the *Berkshire County Eagle*. For the time being, Melville enjoyed what it still offered that was easy and pleasurable—fishing with Malcolm, swimming at the Morewood's lake and simply being out of doors, but in his heart and mind he was no longer content to live there much longer.

By the fall, the Melvilles left Arrowhead and moved into a house on South Street in Pittsfield, a "square old-fashioned house...in the rear of Backus block" as described by their then eleven-year-old son Stanwix.

"This week Wednesday Papa is going to have the first load of things taken up to the new house and I will have vacation when Mamma is up to the new house getting it ready to move into..." Located in town without any distant views of mountains or valleys, the house was a far cry from Arrowhead, with its country charm and breathtaking views, but there is little to suggest the Melvilles were unhappy with the move. A freak carriage accident in November, in which Melville broke several ribs and injured his shoulder, made him wary of all carriage rides from then on, even though he had treasured them so dearly for years before.

A CHANGE OF HANDS

When the farmhouse remained unsold throughout the summer of 1862, it became clear that an independent buyer would not step forward. Allan Melville, looking for a new summer house for his second wife, Jane, offered to buy it from Melville, and a deal between the two men was agreed to privately, apparently without consulting Lizzie, who truly owned Arrowhead in full. Allan would buy just less than half of the original property, including the house and outbuildings, for $3,000, not paying in cash but instead taking it in partial payment for his own house on East Twenty-Sixth Street in New York that Herman and Lizzie would henceforth call home. As Maria suggested, "Herman seems to be much pleased with the prospect. He has always liked New York, & is not the first man who has been beguiled into the country, & found out by experience that it was not the place for him."

Prior to their departure, Lizzie and Herman took a farewell tour and second honeymoon in the Berkshires, a week-long trip that took them to scenic spots like Bash-Bish Falls, Mount Everett and the hill towns of Becket, Savoy and Cummington. It was a successful and bittersweet journey, giving the two of them time alone to reflect on their lives together in the Berkshires and to say goodbye to the countryside. "We passed through some of the wildest and most enchanting scenery, both mountain and valley and I cannot sufficiently congratulate myself that I have seen it before leaving Berkshire," Lizzie exclaimed. Upon their return, a dazzling party hosted by Sarah Morewood at Broadhall to honor Colonel William Francis Bartlett, a Civil War hero who was about to take command of the Massachusetts 57th, concluded with a dramatic fireworks display. It was a celebratory end to their departure, and the final fete hosted by their friend and neighbor

Bash-Bish Falls was one of the scenic spots Lizzie and Herman visited during their farewell tour in the Berkshires.

before she died at the young age of thirty-nine from tuberculosis.

The Melvilles' departure from Pittsfield in the fall of 1863 marked the conclusion of an extraordinary chapter for the author and his family. Herman had arrived thirteen years earlier carrying unshakable confidence in himself as a celebrated author at home and abroad, a progressive and intellectual thinker, a gentleman farmer and family man who was ready to return to his roots in the Berkshires and use its bucolic scenery and his kinship with fellow authors there as inspiration to further his pursuits. Though the Arrowhead years were the most prolific for his writing, Melville's time in the Berkshires proved to be extraordinarily difficult financially, emotionally and physically. By 1863, the place that had held such great promise had become a burden, and the chance to open a new chapter of life in New York seemed like the only logical next step.

In this circa 1870 summer view of the property, neighbor Richard Lathers looks on as members of the family set out on a carriage ride.
Courtesy of The Berkshire Historical Society

9

A RETURN TO NEW YORK

At 44, Herman Melville closed the chapter of his life at Arrowhead and prepared to return to city living, where he would write largely for his own benefit rather than for a public audience. In addition to the much-needed change of scenery, Melville knew an urban life could provide countless educational, cultural and social benefits, if he and his family wished to take advantage of them.

Allan's house was an ample and quiet retreat from the harsher realities of New York City. The brownstone, located at 104 East Twenty-Sixth Street, was spacious by city standards, measuring 20 feet wide and 47 feet long with a narrow back yard stretching 40 feet. Because the house faced north, it did not get much natural light, but it did have plenty of bedrooms for the children, a dining room and parlor for entertaining and room for a small handful of servants. Though the accommodations were not lavish, they were perfectly suitable by most standards.

Allan and Sophia had always been content there. From the beginning of her marriage, however, Allan's second wife Jane Melville made it quite clear that the house was not up to her standards. Coming into the Melville clan with her own fortune, Jane was characterized by everyone in the family as haughty and pretentious. She was all too happy to have her new husband sell the house to his older brother as soon as possible. It was a quick sale arranged between the two men, and although Lizzie might not have been thrilled by a move that would put her at a greater distance from her family in Boston, she could not dispute how important it was to Herman's well-being. With time and some sprucing up, she knew she could call her brother-in-law's former house her own.

Even though Lizzie's inheritance had made it possible for the Melvilles to pay off all their debts in Pittsfield, the $10,750 asking price for the New York house was extravagant, particularly considering once they took possession, they would still need to assume a $7,750 mortgage. Additionally, there were huge expenses to anticipate—updating interiors, employing servants and numerous other household necessities—all of which would add up quickly and take a financial toll. Unless Herman found some sort of steady employment and started contributing to the family income, Lizzie's nest egg would dwindle away quickly.

CIVIL WAR & POETRY

Despite that reality, Melville seemed to feel no great urgency in finding a job right away, and spent the first few years in New York concentrating on his own interests. He reconnected with Evert Duyckinck and other literati who shared his aesthetic interests. He also resumed his long rambling walks along the wharves of the Battery, Central Park and Riverside Park; he read avidly and closely followed the daily news of the victories and losses of Union troops in the ongoing Civil War. He devoted much of his private time to perfecting his poetry. When "The March to the Sea" appeared in the February 1866 issue of *Harper's New Monthly Magazine,* his cousin Kate Gansevoort was delightfully surprised, noting "I have never read any of his poetry before… *This piece* is very inspiring & describes Sherman's Grand March." The poems were mostly short, somber and reflective pieces focusing on the brutal and devastating war.

Critics wrote that though he had "abundant force and fire," "he has written too rapidly…. His poetry runs into the epileptic. His rhymes are fearful." Others summarily declared: "Nature did not make [Melville] a poet."

With several relatives playing important roles in the Union Army, and finding his own daily life profoundly affected by the news from the front, Melville felt an urgency to see the war effort first-hand. He also knew that the experience would give legitimacy to the poems he was interested in writing. In April 1864, Allan joined Melville on a trip to Vienna, Virginia where the two brothers tried to see their cousin Guert Gansevoort, who was commanding the ironclad warship "Roanoke," defending the harbor at Hampton Roads. The experience of seeing the camp and even joining the cavalry for a scouting expedition gave Melville material for several poems, but especially a long narrative entitled "The Scout Toward Aldie." The ensuing Civil War pieces—some 70 poems—later came together as a collection entitled Battle-Pieces and Aspects of the War, published by Harper & Brothers in 1866.

Melville's badge identified him as a custom's inspector for the Port of New York. It was a job he held for twenty years, during which time he never saw a raise to his $4 a day paycheck.
From the Herman Melville Collection
at The Berkshire Athenaeum
Photo by Eric Korenman

When the *New York Herald* listed it as one of Harper's new titles, they noted, "For ten years the public has wondered what has become of Melville." Unfortunately, those curious about the novelist's aptitude for poetry were largely disappointed. Critics wrote that though he had "abundant force and fire," "he has written too rapidly….His poetry runs into the epileptic. His rhymes are fearful." Others summarily declared: "Nature did not make [Melville] a poet." The book of poems was a complete failure; from an edition of 1,260 copies, more than 300 were given to reviewers, and only 486 copies sold in the two years after publication. Rather than making any money from the venture, Melville had lost some $400 on it.

By this time it was abundantly clear to the 47-year-old Melville—and to his family—that to continue pursuing a public writing career would be foolhardy. Even though he had published nine novels and sixteen magazine stories, and his fame from bestselling works like *Typee* and *Omoo* still reverberated ever so distantly, Melville was so completely out of favor with the critics and the public that even he had to admit that he had no sustainable future as a full-time author.

CUSTOMS WORK AT THE PORT OF NEW YORK

At the conclusion of 1866, Melville secured a desk job as a customs inspector for the Port of New York. It was a civil servant, government position, attained largely through the efforts of his wife and family connections. Melville would hold the job of a customs inspector for the next twenty years, working on the docks six days a week, with just national holidays and two weeks off a year, at a modest but adequate salary of $4 a day. In the twenty years he held the position, he never saw a raise.

His job requirements were to check the docking certificates and bills of lading for all incoming vessels, and to inspect cargoes for prohibited imported items—such as illegal animal hides, certain wines and spirits and illegally packaged cigars—as well as to itemize all provisions before they were loaded on departing vessels. He spent countless hours filling out standardized forms and reports on incoming ships. It was mundane and soul-crushing work for a creative, independent spirit, though it might have afforded him time to write quietly during lulls in the schedule of incoming and departing ships.

Throughout all the years he served as a customs officer, Melville never wrote anything about his job—his daily routine, his colleagues, or even anything about the Custom House itself. His silence during these years speaks volumes of his dislike of the work and his sense of failure in himself and his writing career. His depression grew, and there are several indications that he drank heavily during this time, adding to his already strained relationship with Lizzie and the children, who were all old enough to see the ill effects alcohol could have on family life. When his eldest son Malcolm died by his own hand in 1867 (it was never determined if the self-inflicted gun shot was a suicide or accidental), Melville's pain and grief were almost unbearable.

In September 1869, the Melvilles' second son, Stanwix, went to sea, following in his father's footsteps. Like his father, Stanwix was thought to have the "demon of restlessness" and would spend the remainder of his life as a wanderer and a beachcomber, dying alone and unknown in a San Francisco Hospital at age 35. Lizzie's relationship with her husband during these years was so fractured that for a time she strongly considered a divorce—a move that both her family and the family minister wholeheartedly supported, although she ultimately chose to remain with her husband.

RESPITES AT SNUG HARBOR AND ARROWHEAD

With pervasive feelings of gloom, sadness and tension in the New York household, Herman found refuge on Staten Island, where his brother Thomas, now a retired sea captain, had recently been appointed the governor of Snug Harbor, a home for retired merchant seaman located on a scenic, 130-acre

Arrowhead continued to function as a working farm as well as a country retreat after Allan and his wife Jane took possession. In the foreground, Allan oversees haying in the field to the north of the house.

Courtesy of The Berkshire Historical Society

plot of land. Thomas presided over Snug Harbor's community of hundreds of retired or disabled sailors from the elegant Governor's House, a 30-room dwelling with plenty of room for guests. When he could pull himself away from his customs inspector duties, Melville found great pleasure as a guest at the Governor's House, enjoying the bracing salt air and large community of former sailors, who were delighted to trade stories and relive past adventures on the high seas with the famed author of *Typee* and *Omoo*.

Over the following years, Herman and Lizzie also escaped their city life with regular if brief visits to Arrowhead, often during his two-week holidays. Since they had assumed ownership of the property, the Allan Melvilles had made several improvements to "poor simple *Arrowhead*," as Jane described it in a letter to a friend. Unlike Herman and Lizzie, who had never had the financial resources to renovate on a large scale, the new mistress at Arrowhead had plans that included a new front porch, repainting the entire house exterior in a bolder and more fashionable ochre color with brown trim, replacing carpets, putting in a new stove, freshly painting all the rooms, as well as overseeing "purchases of furniture, kitchen utensils, cook-stove &c." With her husband's New York law practice thriving, and her own family money at hand, Jane was equally interested in creating extensive and fashionable gardens befitting a summer residence, noting that "Arrowhead would not be so attractive if I could have no garden."

Her changes did not go unnoticed by visiting family members, and when Maria passed time with Allan and Jane in October of 1865, she exclaimed that "(t)he country looks splendid gorgeous, some of the woods look like a garden of gigantic tulips. Allan has made great improvements here, both within & out of doors—Arrowhead looks like a different place, it is now a beautiful place." Additionally, she was delighted that "Allan has put out a great many Norway pines, & dwarf fruit trees, built a new barn & out houses—laid out new paths &c." With a generous nod to his brother's literary genius which had found a home inside the four walls of the farmhouse, Allan also put his own mark on the interior decoration at Arrowhead. He ornamented the massive center chimney of the old farmhouse with a quotation from his brother's short story "I and My Chimney," which remains visible today, and even hired local Pittsfield photographer C. Seaver to capture an image of the completed work, giving copies of the photo to Lizzie to share with her husband.

The beginning of 1872 was marked by sadness when both Allan Melville, Jr., and his mother Maria both passed away. In an uncharacteristic expression

The Melvilles used the "Chimney Room" as a dining room. It was altered several times, but the inscription from Melville's "I and My Chimney" (1855) above the fireplace was added by Allan Melville as a testament to his brother's writing. The short story begins "I and my chimney, two grey-head-ed old smokers, reside in the country. We are, I may say, old settlers here; particularly my old chimney, which settles more and more every day."

This 18th-century style desk and bookcase can be traced back to the Melvilles' New York brownstone, where they lived from 1863 until Melville's death in 1891. Referred to as "The Billy Budd Desk," many believe Melville used it to write several late works.

From the Herman Melville Collection at The Berkshire Athenaeum

Photo by Eric Korenman

of kindness, Jane encouraged Bessie and Fanny to reunite with their parents at Arrowhead for Herman and Lizzie's silver wedding anniversary the following August. As everyone gathered in Pittsfield, they must have marveled at the changes recent years had brought to Berkshire County and Pittsfield. More and more large summer estates, called "cottages," were dotting the landscape, and wealthy families from New York and Chicago were settling in with their staffs and steady streams of houseguests for a summer season in the country.

All of the Melvilles were particularly delighted to see an old friend become a new neighbor. Wealthy New York lawyer Richard Lathers, who had been a close friend of Allan's, was in the process of putting the final touches on a sprawling new estate just across the road from Arrowhead, where he had amassed acres of open farmland and crowned it with a grand Italianate villa, gardens and statuary. Named Abby Lodge, the house looked large and imposing from the front, but for "those who came into the house from the road, when they stepped through the center door, found themselves still outside upon the very wide spreading piazza, which was like an open room. From this piazza one looked upon a panoramic view, up and down the Housatonic valley."

Bringing old friends and family together, the Melvilles' anniversary was a bittersweet gathering. Though the landscape and the house itself were modernized as the years passed by, for Herman and Lizzie, Arrowhead still reverberated with both fond and melancholy memories as well as powerful associations. The majestic mountain view, especially from the piazza or adjoining parlor, remained a key feature of the family's deep attachment to the property. Herman's niece Florence gave life to the mountain in her own writing, averring that "Nowhere can he be seen to such advantage as from our parlor, where the distant mountain and all the lovely expanse which lies between of velvet lawn sloping to the river's edge, dark woods rustling in the autumn winds and little villages nesting in the valley, are set around by the old window-frame, forming an everpresent, exquisite picture."

LATER YEARS

The final decades of Herman's life fell into a more comfortable rhythm, especially as small inheritances from distant relatives filtered down, giving Herman and Lizzie a level of financial security that made their later years easier. They spent much time in residence with Thomas and Katie at the

Governor's House in Snug Harbor, Herman commuting by ferry to and from work, and leaving their New York house locked up for months at a time.

One of the most meaningful changes in Herman's life was that he was finally able to publish his own work without worry of expense. In every spare moment, he turned his focus to drafting and revising his epic poem *Clarel*, at times tapping back into the writing with the obsessive fury that had characterized his earlier work. The eighteen-thousand line poem, entitled *Clarel: A Poem and Pilgrimmage in the Holy Land*, was inspired by his 1856 travels and was published by G.P. Putnam & Sons in 1876. Yet again, and perhaps not surprisingly by this point, the work was largely ignored by the reading public, and in 1879 Putnam & Sons obtained permission from the author to pulp the unsold copies—some two hundred of the three hundred sets they had printed. Herman also completed a book of poetry for Lizzie entitled *Weeds and Wildings Chiefly: With a Rose or Two*, which was a private and nostalgic book of poems largely about Arrowhead. Roses were Lizzie's favorite flower, and the title suggests a sort of late-life apology to his wife, who had suffered his greatness, his madness and his irascibility for so many years.

At sixty-six, Melville retired from his position at the Customs House, and quietly returned to life at home on East Twenty-Sixth street full time. Though his daughter Fanny had married, daughter Bessie remained with her parents, suffering from a progressive, crippling arthritis that left her largely incapacitated and dependent on care from her parents for the rest of their lives.

The Melvilles' newly comfortable financial circumstances afforded them the chance to freshen up the furnishings on East Twenty-Sixth Street, and they set about brightening the dark house with inherited pieces and nautical prints, to which Melville added considerably with many of his own purchases. He took to studying and collecting prints with a curatorial exactitude, spending hours pouring over them and referencing them in his large personal library. When he felt the strength to do so, he continued to enjoy long walks both in Central Park or along the bluffs of Riverside Park.

A QUIET REDISCOVERY

Looking back on his life from the perch of his 70s, Melville knew that his early admirers were long since gone, either having died or simply forgotten about him after so many years of silence. He had years before decided to

This engraving on wood was done by L. F. Grant and first appeared in Raymond Weaver's biography of Melville *Herman Melville, Mariner and Mystic*, published in 1921. The engraving was made from a 1860 photo of Melville by Pittsfield photographer Rodney H. Dewey.

Courtesy of The Berkshire Athenaeum, Pittsfield, MA

turn inward and focus on writing as his own pursuit, rather than something professional that he could sell to the public. He wrote two more books of poetry, *John Marr* and *Timoleon*, which were each issued in tiny editions of just twenty-five copies and meant to be read only by friends and relatives. He also spun off an idea from one of the poems, developing a story of a sailor confined in chains the night before his execution. Although it remained unfinished at his death, this novella would ultimately become a world-renowned success, known as *Billy Budd, Sailor*. Lizzie discovered the unfinished work hidden in a tin bread box, but decided not to pursue its publication because she worried about more negative reviews. Years later, the unfinished manuscript was rediscovered by Melville's first biographer Raymond M. Weaver in 1919, the centennial anniversary of Melville's birth. With the assistance of Melville's granddaughter Eleanor Metcalf, it was published in 1924.

After being wracked by depression, anxiety, family tragedies, financial insecurities and an unquenchable restlessness, Melville spent his final years in a sort of quiet acceptance of the arc of his career. When his name began to be mentioned here and there—either in Nathaniel Hawthorne's posthumously published notebooks, or in books about Hawthorne's life—a small but curious group of followers began to question what had become of the famous "Typee" author. In England, a younger circle of literati began to write to Melville, and to mention him in magazine articles and newspapers, praising not only *Typee* and *Omoo*, which had always maintained a certain popularity, but also his earlier maligned *Mardi* and the English edition of *The Whale*.

At the time of Herman Melville's death on September 28, 1891, at the age of 72, there were indications that he might one day be remembered as a notable author of the mid-19th century. This was in large part due to the small but significant group of English critics and readers who were ever so softly, but steadily, beginning to sing his praises. Melville could not have imagined, however, that within just a few more decades, he would be considered one of the greatest American prose writers of the 19th century, and that many of his works, especially *Moby-Dick*, *Billy Budd, Sailor* and *Bartleby, The Scrivener* would resonate deeply with critics and readers well into the next two centuries.

Though Melville physically departed the Berkshires at the mid-point of his life, the creative genius he harnessed there sustained him throughout the remainder of his years. It is rare to feel a connection to so distinguished a literary mind over the span of more than a century, but that connection is entirely possible at Arrowhead. Here visitors have an extraordinary opportunity to experience first-hand the inspirational landscape that took hold of Herman Melville at a young age, and fueled his creative spirit until the very last strokes of his pen.

CR

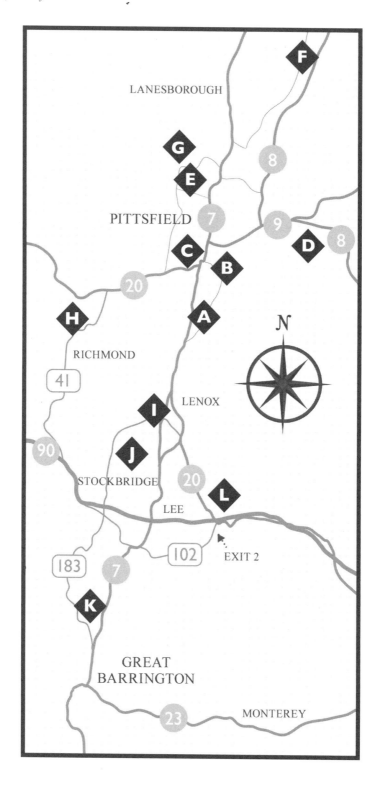

THE MELVILLE TRAIL

Explore the landscapes that inspired Melville by following the Melville Trail. Four of his most beloved places now have permanent interpretive panels: Arrowhead, Pontoosuc Lake, Berkshire Athenaeum and Monument Mountain.

Eight additional places that Melville visited are included—Park Square, Hancock Shaker Village, Crane Museum, Balance Rock, Lenox Court House, Tanglewood/Hawthorne Cottage, October Mountain and, of course, Mount Greylock.

A) ARROWHEAD
780 Holmes Road
Pittsfield, MA   413.442.1793
www.mobydick.org

B) BERKSHIRE ATHENAEUM
1 Wendell Avenue
Pittsfield, MA   413.499.9480
www.pittsfieldlibrary.org

C) PARK SQUARE
1 North Street
Pittsfield, MA
www.downtownpittsfield.com

D) CRANE MUSEUM
40 Pioneer Street
Dalton, MA   413.684.6380
www.crane.com

E) PONTOOSUC LAKE
1400 North Street
Pittsfield, MA
www.discoverpittsfield.com

F) MOUNT GREYLOCK
30 Rockwell Road
Lanesborough, MA   413.499.4262
www.mass.gov

G) BALANCE ROCK STATE PARK
Pittsfield State Forest
www.mass.gov

H) HANCOCK SHAKER VILLAGE
1843 W Housatonic Street
Pittsfield, MA   413.443.0188
www.hancockshakervillage.org

I) LENOX COURT HOUSE
www.lenox.org

J) HAWTHORNE COTTAGE
www.lenox.org

K) MONUMENT MOUNTAIN
Route 7
Gt. Barrington, MA   413.298.3239
www.thetrustees.org

L) OCTOBER MOUNTAIN
256 Woodland Road
Lee, MA   413.243.1778
www.mass.gov

A partnership of the Berkshire Historical Society at Arrowhead, The City of Pittsfield, Berkshire Athenaeum and The Trustees of Reservations, the Melville Trail deepens our understanding of Herman Melville's connection to and love of many places in Berkshire County. The Trail is a collaborative project made possible by a grant from Housatonic Heritage—visit their website to learn even more about this landscape and its history.

LIST OF SOURCES

"Herman Melville's Arrowhead, Manual of Interpretation and Reference Materials", Berkshire Historical Society, 2001.

Parker, Hershel, "Herman Melville," *American National Biography*, Volume 15. Ed. By John A. Garraty and Mark C. Carnes. New York, Oxford: Oxford University Press, 1999.

Parker, Hershel, "Herman Melville," *American History Illustrated* (September/October, 1991): 28-47.

Parker, Hershel, *Herman Melville A Biography, Volume 1, 1819-1851*. Baltimore and London: The John Hopkins University Press, 1966.

Parker, Hershel, *Herman Melville A Biography, Volume 2, 1851-1891*. Baltimore and London: The John Hopkins University Press, 2002.

Phillips, John A. "Melville Meets Hawthorne: How a Champagne Picnic on Monument Mountain Led to a Profound Revision of *Moby-Dick* and Disenchantment," *American Heritage* 27, no 1 (December 1975): 16-21, 87-90.

Robertson-Lorant, Laurie, *Melville, A Biography*. New York: Clarkson Potter, 1996.

Updike, John "Reflections, Melville's Withdrawl." *The New Yorker* (May 10, 1982):120-147.